THE KISTE AND OGAN SOCIAL CHANGE
SERIES IN ANTHROPOLOGY

Editors

ROBERT C. KISTE   EUGENE OGAN

University of Minnesota

Frank C. Miller was born in Quincy, Illinois. After completing his undergraduate work at Carleton College, he was enrolled in graduate work at Harvard University, where his doctorate was awarded in 1960.

A teaching appointment at Carleton was followed by his move to the University of Minnesota, where he served first as Assistant Dean of International Programs and then as chairman of the Anthropology Department for three years. Dr. Miller is currently on sabbatical from the University of Minnesota, working under a senior fellowship from the National Endowment for Humanities; he is engaged in studying and writing about new towns such as the one described in this book.

Dr. Miller's specializations and interests include social and cultural change, urbanization, Middle America, Amerindians, and the methods and theories of social anthropology. Among his current professional memberships are the American Anthropological Association, the American Ethnological Society, and the Latin American Studies Association.

OLD VILLAGES AND A NEW TOWN

 Cummings Publishing Company

Industrialization in Mexico

FRANK C. MILLER

University of Minnesota

Menlo Park, California · Reading, Massachusetts
London · Amsterdam · Don Mills, Ontario · Sydney

Cummings Publishing Company, Inc.
2727 Sand Hill Road
Menlo Park, California 94025

Foreword

Dr. Frank C. Miller's study is one of the initial volumes in Cummings' series of ethnographic case studies on social and cultural change. With the exception of a few small populations in the most remote regions of the earth, no society today remains unaffected by other social groups and by the stream of current world events. The studies comprising this series reflect this basic state of modern man's condition and they focus on a common theme: the ways in which members of contemporary societies respond to and develop strategies for coping with modifications of their social and/or physical environments.

Each study in the series is based on field research by the author. In addition to focusing on the theme of the series, each author is encouraged to develop other relevant theoretical implications of his material. Studies from the major geographical and cultural areas of the world will be represented in forthcoming volumes, and the series will provide a fairly balanced consideration of literate and nonliterate societies. It is hoped that the series will also provide the materials from which some generalizations and conclusions about the processes of social and cultural change may be generated.

This particular study is concerned with a large-scale project in planned social and cultural change. In the early 1950's, a valley not far from Mexico City was selected as the site for a new industrial complex and town. For centuries, the valley had been a relatively unimportant region of Mexico; it possessed few natural resources of value, and it was occupied by a number of rather traditional peasant communities whose inhabitants struggled to gain even a meagre livelihood from the land. Professor Miller outlines the history of the region and its inhabitants, beginning with the sixteenth century when large haciendas were the dominant social and economic institutions throughout most of Mexico; he also examines the Mexican Revolution and the social reforms which followed it, and he describes in detail the more recent processes involved in creating the wholly new industrial town.

For the residents of the valley, the project has represented a massive exposure to modern technology and to unfamiliar forms of social organization. It has also made available new alternatives to traditional lifestyles and has engendered the hope of a more prosperous existence. Professor Miller discusses the people's perceptions of the new town and carefully examines the variety of their responses to such a major alteration of their total environment. His own analysis of the images and concepts pertaining to peasant villages leads him to scrutinize and to raise questions about the work of Robert Redfield, Oscar Lewis, and other pioneers of anthropological research among rural populations in Mexico. Further, the concept of "the image of limited good" which has been so well articulated by George Foster, and which is often assumed to be an integral part of the world view of peasant villagers, is examined in a situation which does not bind people to lifeways of the past.

While the study is addressed primarily to issues which have been of interest to students of anthropology, its findings are potentially relevant to other programs which involve urban planning and economic development. As Professor Miller reports, the project has not fulfilled all of the expectations of its designers. It is possible that certain variables which have prevented the full realization of certain goals could not have been foreseen. The achievement of other goals, however, might well have been facilitated if studies such as this one were more common and more widely disseminated. All efforts at directed social and cultural change are beset with a great many potential pitfalls, and it is only through careful examination of man's current and past efforts to improve his lot that humans may learn to shape more successfully the decisions and events which influence the quality of their lives.

Other volumes in the Cummings' series, notably, David Jacobson's *Itinerant Townsmen: Friendship and Social Order in Urban Uganda*, will be of interest to students concerned with the anthropology of urban life and complex societies.

University of Minnesota ROBERT C. KISTE
Minneapolis, Minnesota EUGENE OGAN
September, 1972 *Series Editors*

Acknowledgments

Many people contributed to the research on which this book is based and to the shaping of the manuscript. I would like to thank all of them, and especially the following: Bert Pelto for methodological inspiration; Bob Kiste, Steve Gudeman, and John Ingham, for congenial colleagueship and excellent suggestions for improvements in the first draft; Frank and Ruth Young, for sharing their ideas and their data; Willard Cochrane, who was Dean of International Programs at the University of Minnesota when the project was funded; Bob Holt, Director of that university's Center for Comparative Studies, for multidisciplinary stimulation and financial support; Fernando Cámara, Rafael Núñez, and Don Winkelmann, an admirable group of consultants; Luis Leñero and Pablo Pindas, for their skill with surveys and their gracious hospitality; John Azer, Gerald Gold, Charles Mundale, John Poggie, Tim Roufs, Jay Schensul, and Barbara Simon, an exceptional group of graduate students; and Nancy Hanson, for her expert typing and sharp eye for awkward phrases.

As the reader will notice, I have drawn extensively on the work of some of the Minnesota graduate students. Their roles are described in Chapter 1, and their relevant writings appear in the bibliography. This book touches on only certain aspects of their collective work: they will be heard from increasingly in the future.

From my own theoretical perspective, I have attempted to fit the pieces into a coherent pattern. I alone am responsible for the conclusions that I draw and for any deficiencies in this book.

My debt to my remarkable wife, Cynthia Cone, cannot be expressed readily in words. She, too, was a graduate student when I was working on the Mexican materials, and her analysis of some of the data was both rapid and insightful. She also drew the maps and helped with matters of organization and style. Within the domain of scholarship and far beyond, she has made many things possible.

Minneapolis, Minnesota   FRANK C. MILLER
September, 1972

FOR
Binny, Peter, Margery, Richard,
Robin, and Emily

Contents

Illustrations

PHOTOGRAPHS

MAPS

CHAPTER ONE

Introduction

In 1955 a new town arose in a barren valley northeast of Mexico City. It is a project of the Mexican Government, an experiment in decentralization and regional development. The local people did not seek this massive intrusion of modern technology and bureaucracy; but it has become, in many ways, the major fact of their existence. It has kindled new hopes and new possibilities for the frustration of those hopes.

This book is about the responses of the people who live in the towns and villages of the impoverished region where the new town is located. To understand their attitudes and behavior, it is no longer sufficient—if it ever was—to analyze the cultural patterns and the social organization of the community. It is necessary to acknowledge the role of policies of state and national governments, for those policies deeply affect the availability of education, opportunities for employment, and other resources which sustain the vitality of the local community.

The new town, which I shall call "Ciudad Industrial," has not fulfilled the great expectations for its own development that accompanied its creation; but it has had an unexpected impact on the towns and villages of the region.[1] It has created a new basis for survival, even for modest prosperity, in communities that had been on the decline. Along with other developments in modern Mexico, it has also created new opportunities

[1] The names of all people and places are pseudonyms.

for individuals to enjoy the fruits of the long struggle known as the Mexican Revolution.

In this book I attempt something more than a descriptive account of the regional impact of the new town. First of all, I shall explain the principles which guided the research, because I feel that they provide a useful model for studies of large-scale development projects. These principles are exemplified throughout the book. Second, I shall present a point of view about the effects of rapid technological change and about the adaptive strategies that people use to cope with it. Rapid change is often described as an "ordeal" or "turmoil" by those who assume that a state of equilibrium is the "normal" state of society. Granting the difficulties of defining what is normal, I think that it makes more sense to assume that change is normal and to concentrate our efforts on understanding how people deal with it. Finally, I shall argue that much anthropological research on Mexico and many anthropological views about the alleged traditionalism of peasants, have created a popular image of the "Mexican village" that applies to only a small proportion of communities in that country, and that applies less and less to even that small proportion as Mexico modernizes. I hope that this book will contribute to a more balanced view of village life in modern Mexico.

History and Setting

The people of the Valley of Los Llanos, located in the State of Hidalgo, have participated in some of the great movements of Mexican history: the cultural confrontation of Indian and Spaniard; the development of the system of *haciendas* or "landed estates"; the agony and triumph of the Revolution; and the accelerating modernization of recent years.

The ruins of a small pyramid in the town of Cerro Grande give testimony to close ties with the great ceremonial center of Teotihuacán, whose two famous pyramids were the symbolic center of a flourishing population long before the arrival of the Spanish conquerors, the vanguard of European culture. While the fortunes of Teotihuacán rose and fell, the Valley of Los Llanos continued to be well-populated. When the conquerors arrived in 1519, twenty thousand Indians lived in the northern part of the valley around what is now Cerro Grande. The present town was one of the first two communities founded by Cortés in Mexico, and was the site of an important early monastery. After 1540 the Valley of Los Llanos and its environs rapidly became a cattle-raising center. The intensive contact between Indian and Spaniard entailed by these developments led to the rapid acculturation of the Indian population, so that today there are no inhabitants in the valley who identify themselves as Indians.[2]

During the next phase of their history, beginning in the seventeenth century, the people of Los Llanos worked on some of the grandest haciendas in all of Mexico. These estates specialized in the production of *pulque*, the traditional drink made from the fermented sap of the *maguey* cactus (known in the United States as the century plant). With the growth of a large and stable market in the capital city, the haciendas flourished; but the fruits of the labor of thousands of workers went principally to build grand houses, both on the haciendas and in Mexico City, and to support the lavish life styles of the owners. The Revolution was fought to eliminate the exploitation that was inherent in the hacienda system, and although it succeeded in certain ways, it did not solve the economic problems of the peasants, particularly of those in the *pulque*-producing regions. They watched the decline of their traditional

---

[2] This point requires further explanation. In Mexico, Indians are defined in cultural rather than racial terms. About ten percent of the national population consider themselves to be Indians: they speak an Indian language (and frequently Spanish as well), follow an Indian culture, and usually live in a community that is predominantly Indian. They also, of course, have distinctively Indian physical characteristics, but these are shared to some degree by most of the rest of the population because there has been a great deal of genetic mixture. Consequently, these people are usually called *mestizos* ("halfbreeds" or "hybrids") in anthropological literature. The label is unsatisfactory for several reasons: it frequently has derogatory connotations, it is not often used in everyday speech, and it carries the connotation of racial mixture when the important thing about the category is that it is culturally defined. It would be better to call these people what they call themselves: *Mexicanos* ("Mexicans"). Some are dark-skinned and some light; some are traditional and some modern; but all have an increasingly strong sense of national identity.

economy as public preferences shifted to beer and soft drinks. During the 1940's, when rapid industrialization was beginning in the rest of Mexico, the Valley of Los Llanos was suffering increasingly severe economic problems. To combat the growing poverty, the national government built three large factories and a new town to house their employees. This ambitious project is a highly visible intrusion of modern industrial society.

The national importance of the *pulque* haciendas and Ciudad Industrial is suggested by the fact that *Artes de México*, a handsomely-designed and profusely illustrated magazine, has devoted a full issue to each topic. The issue on the new town speaks in glowing terms about the "unsuspected beauty" of the area and about the historic and artistic qualities of the colonial churches and the more elegant haciendas. Others have remarked that the Valley of Los Llanos (see Plate 1) suffers from the barrenness of the terrain and the inhospitality of the climate, which is dry, windy, and rather chilly for Mexico. Perhaps for these reasons, it is not one of the most studied areas in Mexico, for the most studied are also the most scenic. It has neither the mystery of Lake Pátzcuaro brooding in the rainy season, the spectacle of the cliffs looming above Tepoztlán, nor the color and diversity of the Indian country in the Highlands of Chiapas. Yet there is beauty in the starkness of the landscape, in the simplicity of the rows of *maguey,* and in the mist over the barley fields before sunrise.

The valley is a crescent-shaped basin surrounded by low mountains, extending roughly from San Manuel in the northeast to Los Llanos in the southeast, bending around a 9,800 foot mountain on the way (see Map 1). Since the valley floor lies at 8,000 feet, the mountain is a mere hill compared to thousands of impressive peaks in Mexico. The basin floor is almost perfectly flat, and most of the settlements are located on the gentle slopes of the mountains, in order not to use up any valuable agricultural land.

The geography of the valley is important for two reasons. In the first place, limited natural resources impose constraints on economic possibilities and therefore on the kinds of lives people can lead. For example, there are definite limits on the potential for agriculture. Level land suitable for mechanized farming is found only in the floor of the valley; and crop yields are

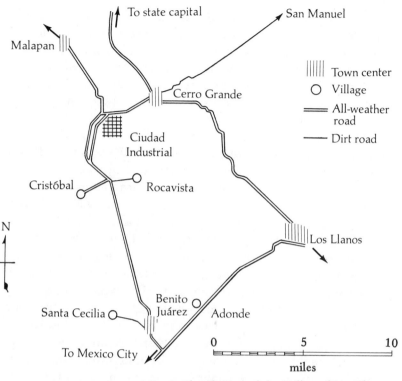

Map 1. Sketch-map of the Valley of Los Llanos.

limited, sometimes drastically, by the scarcity of rain. Secondly, people see the valley as a geographic unit which is distinct from adjacent valleys. Although the whole place may look barren and uninteresting to an outsider accustomed to the natural drama of other parts of Mexico, the residents perceive, in various locales, considerable variation in sun, wind, and mountainside.

Just as the valley is a geographic unit, the communities in it form a network of social and economic ties. Most of the people conduct most of their activities within that network: that is where they live, work, go to market, find their spouses, and raise their children. Unlike many isolated areas of Mexico, the Valley of Los Llanos is intimately connected with the wider society, and especially with the bustling, vital pivot of that society, Mexico City. Although most of the residents visit that cosmopolitan metropolis, some with surprising frequency, the Los Llanos network is nevertheless the immediate context of people's lives.

One of the themes of this book is the importance of a regional perspective for understanding the impact of the new town and its factories. Later in the book I shall argue that a study of social and cultural changes stimulated by this development project must be a regional study, for some of the greatest changes have occurred, not in the new town at all, but in the surrounding communities.

The towns and villages in the Valley of Los Llanos are located in four *municipios*: Cerro Grande, Malapan, Benito Juárez, and Los Llanos. The *municipio* is the local political and territorial division of the states in the Mexican federal system. It is often described as a county; but it is more like a New England township, at least insofar as it is small and all settlements within it are closely tied to the principal one, which can be called the head town or the town center. The *municipio* is of great symbolic significance to most rural Mexicans; it is *mi tierra* ("my land") in the sense of "my own true place of origin." The township is not of great administrative significance; so it is not, after all, very similar to a township or county in the United States. It has little taxing power and therefore does not have the money to build its own schools and public utilities. Decisions about investment in such facilities are made in cooperation with state and federal governments, and the latter is the main source of funds.

Conduct of the Research

This book is based on a research project conducted in the Valley of Los Llanos during 1966-1970. Pertti J. Pelto and I directed the project; the participants included several colleagues in Mexico and many students from Mexican institutions and from the University of Minnesota. A full description of the complexity of the research would encumber the progress of this book, but I would like to explain some of the principles that guided the conduct of the work.

Defining the Input. Even though change is a continuous process, it is useful to study it by identifying a major innovation, technological or otherwise, which is highly visible and whose content can be described clearly. Too many studies

Plate 1.   The Valley of Los Llanos

Plate 2.   A village street (photo by Timothy Roufs)

of change have referred to "the influence of the outside world," without knowing of what that influence consists. In developing societies, highly visible innovations are likely to be sponsored by government programs of one sort or another. Concentrating research on such programs has a double advantage: the goals and methods can be clearly specified, and some useful knowledge and practical wisdom about their effects can be accumulated.

Ciudad Industrial is nothing if not highly visible, and it greatly simplifies the problem of defining "the influence of the outside world." It does not entirely solve the problem, because education and the mass media are also potent influences; we have therefore attempted to deal with them as well.

The Need for Baseline Data. Defining the input does little good if the state of the system receiving the input is unknown. Many studies lack adequate baseline data: they rely on official statistics, which may be inaccurate or at best partially irrelevant; or they rely on the memories of people in the research area, which share the same defects. Research in developing societies seldom has available baseline data collected by social scientists at the *beginning* of basic changes: change is usually studied after the fact. One of the principal reasons that we chose Ciudad Industrial as a site was the earlier research of Frank and Ruth Young, conducted during 1957-1958 and published in an impressive series of articles (Young and Young 1960, 1962, 1966, among others). They had collected extensive data on both communities and individuals, and they generously made it available to us. We repeated many of their interview items point-for-point, in order to have exactly comparable data. This book deals with some of the resulting comparisons; others have been or will be published elsewhere (Miller and Pelto n.d; Poggie and Miller 1969).

A Variety of Methods. To understand the dynamic, complex situation in the Valley of Los Llanos requires a kind of research that is rather different from typical anthropological study. Anthropology is a rapidly changing discipline, so it is risky to generalize about what is typical; but it is probably safe to say that the most common sort of research in cultural anthropology still consists primarily of a year of field work in a single community. The three principal techniques of field work are participant observation, informal interviewing, and systematic interviewing of key informants. In participant observation, the investigator is the research instrument: he records data about cultural patterns while participating in the events of everyday life. At the same time he may "interview" people simply by engaging them in conversation. This sort of approach leads gradually to systematic work with key informants, individuals who have specialized knowledge by virtue of their social roles or personal characteristics.

In the Los Llanos research, the traditional techniques of anthropological research were employed, but we did not think that they alone would generate sufficient data to answer some of the broad questions we had. For this reason we also relied rather heavily on survey techniques. The social survey is a standard procedure in most social sciences, especially in political science and sociology, and it is being used increasingly in anthropology. One of our largest data-gathering operations was a survey of households in seven towns and villages, carried out in the summer of 1967 by a Mexican research institute. The communities included the four that had been studied earlier by the Youngs, plus three more that were included to represent a wider range of economic patterns and different trends of change. The sample consisted of both husbands and wives in 475 households, giving a total of 950 interviews. Additional information about the survey will be presented in later chapters when some of the results are discussed.

Individual field workers used methods that were appropriate to their interests and their needs for data. John J. Poggie, Jr. (1968-1972) combined the survey technique with the use of key informants: he conducted a survey of key informants in 40 communities, and thereby efficiently obtained much of the information needed for his study of the network. For a study of the aspirations of school children, Timothy Roufs (1971) administered a questionnaire in all sixth grades and in all secondary schools in the region. A written questionnaire would not be an appropriate technique for a sample of adults because of the average level of literacy; but it is useful, when one has the cooperation of the teachers, for obtaining information about a large number of school children.

Barbara Simon (1972), in an intensive investigation of social stratification in a single community, relied largely on standard methods of field work; she supplemented these with a special interviewing technique for the study of prestige, which will be described in Chapter 8. Changing patterns of education in the same community were studied by Jean Schensul (1972), who conducted systematic interviews with teachers and with samples of both students and parents, in addition to using participant observation and informal interviewing. The research of Charles Mundale (1971), a political scientist, was also most amenable to the methods of field work. He was interested in local politics and its role in the integration of region, state, and nation, and such a sensitive subject is better investigated by field work than by surveys.

Our overall research strategy was what Pelto (1940:44) has called "the quantitative-qualitative mix." The techniques of field work were used to provide data of richness and depth, and surveys and other systematic methods were used to add dimensions of reliability and comparability.

International Cooperation. The present debate about the ethics of research and the international role of social scientists from the United States (see Beals 1969) was just beginning when we started our research in Mexico. Nevertheless, we were concerned about the tendency of social scientists to be "intellectual imperialists," to "mine" foreign areas for data and to take the "profits" home, leaving nothing in the host country. We wanted to plan our research so that it would contribute something to Mexico and to Mexican social science, and we also wanted to draw on the resources of the scholarly community there. In the hope of accomplishing this, we engaged a group of consultants who assisted us greatly in the conduct of the research, and we informed them fully about our goals and sources of financial support. The consultants included Fernando Cámara Barbachano, an anthropologist who served as administrator of Ciudad Industrial during 1960-1964, and who is now Sub-Director of the *Instituto Nacional de Antropología e Historia*; Rafael Nuñez Ovando, a psychologist at the *Universidad de Los Américas*; Donald Winkelmann, a North American economist who was teaching in the post-graduate center for agricultural economics at the National School of Agriculture; and Luis Leñero Otero, sociologist, Director of the School of

Social and Political Sciences at the *Universidad Ibero-Americana*, and Director of the *Instituto Mexicano de Estudios Sociales* (IMES).

The most extensive relationships we developed were with IMES, a private, non-profit research institute. (A literal translation of the name would be misleading: *estudios sociales* means "social research," not "social studies" as these phrases are used in the United States.) With great skill and efficiency, IMES pre-tested the interview schedule and carried out the survey of households. A team of about a dozen well-trained interviewers, under the supervision of Pablo Pindas, conducted almost one thousand interviews during the course of three weeks. In the smaller communities the interviewing was completed in a day. One advantage of such rapid work is that little time is available for the spread of rumors and misinformation about the purposes of the survey.

The IMES team coded the data, and IBM cards were punched at the University of Minnesota. Duplicate sets of cards were deposited with IMES and with the National Museum of Anthropology, so that the data would be available immediately in Mexico.

A Multidisciplinary Perspective. A regional study of the impact of a new town is a rather ambitious undertaking which must draw on the resources of several disciplines. The multidisciplinary aspect of the research was greatly facilitated by the University of Minnesota's Center for Comparative Studies in Technological Development and Social Change, under the leadership of Robert T. Holt, Professor of Political Science. This institutional framework contributed to the research in two ways: it coordinated the participation of anthropologists, economists, political scientists, psychologists, and sociologists; and it furnished an informal forum for the exchange of ideas about both method and theory in the study of modernization.

The Problem of Technology

Industrialization and other forms of technological change are currently the subject of much controversy; and the role of technology in social and cultural change has long been the focus of scholarly dispute. Since this book is about a situation in which technology is the most important stimulus for change, I want to state, as succinctly as possible, my views about the question of determinism. Determinism, in simple language, is the doctrine that things or events are determined; that is, they have to be the way they are because certain laws or forces make them that way. Anthropology has existed as a discipline for more than 100 years, and its history has involved many fundamental arguments about environmental, technological, racial, cultural, and other doctrines of determinism. I deliberately use the term "doctrine" rather than "theory" because I consider these arguments to be philosophical disputes about basic assumptions, not debates about scientific theories that can be verified or rejected by empirical evidence.

Throughout this book I emphasize both the opportunities and the constraints imposed by rapid technological change, but I do not advance a doctrine of technological determinism. Technology sets limits which are more confining than many people would like to think, but within those limits there is scope for human creativity. More important, technology itself is a product of human creativity and is subject to change. Today there is growing concern that a runaway technology will destroy its creator. I share these concerns, but I also want to emphasize that they are by their very nature most common in the most highly industrialized societies. Many developing societies believe that they must accelerate the development of their technology if they are ever to avoid domination by industrial giants and to narrow the gap that is growing between the rich nations and the poor. A Mexican villager who can make six times as much on an automobile assembly line as on the farm is not likely to worry over the dangers of the internal combustion engine.

Adaptive Strategies

The villagers of Los Llanos, like most people in the world, are in the position of reacting to events that are determined by outside forces. They have witnessed the rise and fall of the *pulque* haciendas; the coming of the Revolution, with schools and land reform; and the growth of Ciudad Industrial, built by government agencies in accordance with decisions made in Mexico City. The coming of industry has brought new opportunities for individual careers and for the survival of communities. I shall analyze the responses to these opportunities in terms of the concept of adaptive strategies, or plans for adjusting behavior to the requirements of changing circumstances.

In the changing circumstances of the Valley of Los Llanos, the two most important elements are new schools and new jobs. Chapter 8 will be concerned, among other things, with the role of education in the sorting-out process that allocates individuals to new occupations, especially those connected with the factories. Chapter 9 will examine the educational system and the effects that it has had on the aspirations of the people.

Strategies for coping with these new circumstances have required more conscious planning by more people than ever before. Parents, together with their children, decide whether or not to invest some of the family's resources in a high school education, perhaps the first in the family. Individuals decide whether or not to seek new jobs in the factories, where the environment is strange and forbidding.

With new choices have come new constraints as well. Economic development has opened up possibilities, and the schools and the mass media have communicated them all too well. The result is that aspirations have risen to a level that the system is unable to satisfy. Many parents want a high school education for their children, yet places in each school are severely limited. Many high school students aspire to professional careers, but only a minute percentage will attain their goals. The problems have been compounded by a high rate of population growth: a new generation of young people, more numerous than ever, is putting great pressure on the resources of the system. The strategies of the future will have to come to terms with the constraints as well as with the choices.

CHAPTER TWO

_____

The Hacienda and the Revolution

Haciendas increasingly dominated the life of rural Mexicans from the sixteenth century until the Revolution of 1910. They were the principal institution of both economic and social organization. The hacienda system developed as a means of mobilizing the labor of a rural population oriented primarily toward subsistence agriculture. It adapted to the chronic depression of the seventeenth century and later to the greatly fluctuating demand for certain agricultural commodities. Before the Revolution, about half the rural population lived on haciendas. The traditional form of the system was destroyed by the Revolution, but today some Mexican intellectuals are offering increasing criticism of new forms of concentration of land.

The Hacienda as a Social System

The hacienda was, to use a current phrase, a "total institution." Largely self contained, it encompassed the entire social horizons of most of its occupants. Eric Wolf (1959:204-8) has written an insightful summary of the fundamental structural principles and the mode of operation of the hacienda. He points out the contradictions inherent in the system: oriented to the market, it often planned to have little to sell; greedy for land, it was careless in the use of it; staffed by large numbers of laborers, it emphasized a personal relationship

17

between worker and owner; devoted to making a profit, it
expended much of its resources in "conspicuous and unpro-
ductive displays of wealth."

The institution of the hacienda has sometimes been called
"feudal" because landless laborers were dependent upon the
rule of a landowner who was almost omnipotent. They thereby
attained a degree of security, but that security depended upon
the good will of the master. The workers did not have the kinds
of legal guarantees which protected the position of the feudal
serf. Wolf's view is that the hacienda was a transitional
institution, part feudal, part capitalist, "caught between past
and future."

The system was an adaptation to the state of chronic
depression. In the Mexico of the seventeenth and eighteenth
centuries, the national market for agricultural products was
small, and it expanded slowly and unsteadily. Towns and
mining camps needed food, but they represented only a small
proportion of the population. Among the rest of the population, almost all of those not located on landed estates were
involved in subsistence agriculture, and they raised all of their
own food. The transportation system was rudimentary, which
meant that surplus from an area with a good harvest could not
be transported cheaply enough or rapidly enough to relieve
shortages in other areas.

Haciendas were commercial operations in that they produced for whatever market existed; but they were also
self-sufficient entities which did not depend for survival upon
the vagaries of the market. Whenever necessary, they could
retreat behind their defenses and live on their own resources.

In Wolf's analysis, another contradiction in the system was
the attitude toward land. Estates used land inefficiently, yet
they were greedy for more. They did not want more land in
order to increase production, because they never aimed at
maximum output. They did not want to control land for its
own sake, but rather to control the labor of people who lived
on it. Subsistence farmers, whether Indians or not, are by
definition largely self-sufficient. They raise their own food and
are not inclined to enter the agricultural labor market except by
necessity. The problem of the hacienda was to mobilize a large
labor force at some times—planting and harvest every year, and

especially in years when the market for cash crops was good—without having to support it year-round. Through the centuries, the solution to the problem was to take over the land by both legal and illegal means, and to let the occupants continue to use it for raising their crops and animals, as long as they worked a certain number of days per week on the lands of the owner.

The workers were tied to the hacienda by various means of coercion, classic in their simplicity and always involving some form of debt-bondage. Workers were advanced small sums of money or offered credit at the company store. They then found it impossible to pay off the debt, since they had virtually no cash income. They were paid, not in money, but in the use of a small plot of hacienda land. On that land they raised food for their families, not commodities for the market. The legal code provided that debts be passed from father to son, which guaranteed a stable supply of labor over the generations.

A large and steady source of cheap labor allowed the owners of the larger estates to live a life of grandeur. They emulated the Spanish nobility and aspired to imitate the graceful life as it was lived in Castile. To the extent that their means permitted, they built grand houses, rode fine horses, and wore beautiful clothes. Such displays of wealth reinforced the owner's dominance over his workers and served as a validation of his high social status.

The bond between owner and worker was a classical example of what anthropologists call a "patron-client relationship." As a matter of fact, in Spanish the owner was called *patrón*, which means much more than simply "patron" in everyday English: it carries the connotation of "boss, protector, and master," although the strength of that connotation varies with the situation. As the terms suggest, the bond between patron and client was more than a relationship between employer and employee in the modern labor market. It was not limited to the economic realm, and it conveyed advantages to both parties. The owner was guaranteed a stable supply of cheap labor and of people to show him great respect and deference. The workers received a degree of economic security and the psychological satisfaction of association with an elegant estate that lent some glamour and dignity to their barren lives.

However, the system also exacted social and psychological costs. The workers were dependent on the grace of the owner for their economic security and psychological satisfaction. Their benefits, such as they were, were not written into any contract grounded in a set of laws to protect the rights of labor. Since they were not related to the owner by a contract, it might seem that they were bound by a personal tie, but Wolf argues to the contrary. He says that the relationship was "personalized" rather than "personal," that it was one which "bears the guise of a personal relation but serves an impersonal function." Haciendas did not exist to provide satisfactions within relationships or to take account of obligations of friendship or kinship. They existed to make a profit and, not incidentally, to support the *patrón* and his family in elegant style. The security furnished by the owner might become ephemeral, and the deference given by the workers was spurious: "a show of humility, a pantomime of servitude."

Even today in the villages of Los Llanos, some elderly people of humble status display that "pantomime of servitude" toward those of elevated position. In rural Mexico generally, interaction between higher and lower is characterized by ritualized politeness and careful deference.

Pre-Revolutionary Social Stratification

The hacienda was not simply an economic arrangement for agricultural production; it was one of the principal institutions in a system of social stratification. Wealth, power, and prestige are unevenly distributed in all human societies. When that distribution is the basis for a ranking of families that carries over from one generation to the next, whether or not there are clearly defined social classes, then a system of stratification is considered to be present. From Karl Marx through Max Weber to the present day, there have been great disagreements about the nature of stratification, but most investigators agree that it is the basic structural principle of complex societies, whether agricultural or industrial.

The hacienda system involved a tremendous concentration of land in the hands of a few. At the time of the Revolution, the top 1 percent of the population owned 19 percent of the land, while the bottom 96 percent owned only 1 percent (Stavenhagen 1970). Some of the estates were almost unbelievably large: one encompassed seventeen villages. Tannenbaum reports that the railroad passed through one hacienda in the State of Hidalgo for a distance of ninety miles; and that the State of Morelos, which is about twice as large as Rhode Island, belonged to thirty-two families (1950:137).

The type of society represented by pre-Revolutionary Mexico is frequently depicted as a pyramid, with a small elite at the peak and a broad mass of peasants at the bottom. The image is useful if we keep in mind that the middle levels were hardly larger than the top. People in commerce, crafts, and services were few because there was no mass market. Peasants consumed little beyond what they produced themselves, so the middle levels produced principally for the elite and for themselves.

Another important feature of traditional Mexico was the relative lack of opportunity for rising to a higher social level. One reason was simply the small size of the elite, compared to great masses of simple country people. A more fundamental reason was inherent in a general feature of peasant societies, a feature that has been described by Fallers (1964:242). Occupations were imbedded in and limited by the social structure. A man's work was carried out on his land or within his household. Farmers, craftsmen, and most tradesmen operated within the family as within a firm. Their sons learned from them and carried on in their fathers' footsteps. For most people there was neither an educational system nor a labor market beyond the family. The opportunities for moving out of that context were extremely limited.

Agriculturally-based civilizations of the sort represented by traditional Mexico are among the least equalitarian in human history. The deep inequalities, based in part on the concentration of land in the hands of a few, were an important source of the 1910 Revolution.

The Mexican Revolution

Any revolution is a product of history, and I shall make no attempt to summarize the complex history that produced the Mexican Revolution. Nevertheless, it is essential to consider its principal causes: the uneven distribution of land; resentment of the dictatorship of Porfirio Díaz and some of his policies; and, indirectly, incipient industrialization.

The Díaz regime lasted from 1876 to 1911, one year after the rebellion began. One of its policies was to allow massive foreign ownership of land and to encourage foreign investment in transportation and industry. In 1910, foreigners, mainly North Americans, owned twenty percent of all privately owned land in the Republic, and forty-three percent in one of the northern states. Although under Díaz haciendas came increasingly to dominate the rural economy, he also laid some of the technological foundation for a modern society. During his dictatorship railroad trackage increased from 666 to 19,280 kilometers (built and owned by foreign companies, of course). Mining prospered; and some light industry, such as textiles, developed rapidly.

The Díaz regime contained some of the seeds of its own destruction. As so often happens in human affairs, basic social trends culminated in events unforeseen by the people who guided and encouraged those trends: the growing encroachment on peasant, especially Indian, lands by the great estates fueled the discontent of the dispossessed; and industrialization began to create a new middle class of managers, professionals, and technicians, who came to resent foreign ownership and dictatorial repression.

These two currents converged to create one of the most thoroughgoing revolutions of the twentieth century. There was no single vanguard, nor a unified ideology or program. Emiliano Zapata, the agrarian leader, joined forces with Francisco Madero, a liberal estate owner from the north. The Revolution was as long as it was thorough. Assassinations, rebellions, and counter-rebellions kept the nation in turmoil for more than a decade. Finally, in 1924, the situation stabilized somewhat, although some of the most significant changes did not take place until the presidential term of Lázaro Cárdenas in 1934-1940.

The Program of the Revolution

Although there was no coherent ideology at the outset, a set of goals and a program to accomplish them emerged over the years. Initially, the major goals were embodied in the slogan of Zapata: *Tierra y Libertad* ("Land and Liberty"). Land meant the redistribution of the holdings of the large estates, and liberty meant an end to dictatorship and economic domination by foreign interests.

The social invention for accomplishing the land reform was the *ejido*, a type of agrarian community named after the traditional communal lands in Indian cultures. In modern *ejidos*, ownership of land rests in the community, so that land cannot legally be sold or rented. Some modern *ejidos* devoted to commercial agriculture operate collectively, but most are composed of small farmers, many producing primarily for subsistence. In such cases, use rights to plots of land are assigned to individuals and may be passed from father to son. The political structure of the agrarian community is defined by the national agrarian code, but the actual mode of operation varies according to local tradition.

The *ejido* replaced the hacienda as the dominant social form in rural Mexico. The new system gave the peasant and small farmer freedom from the exploitative arrangements of the old estates, and a sense of independence derived from membership in a community with inalienable rights to land. It did not solve the problem of rural poverty. That problem is not simply a matter of land tenure; but rather a result of the poverty of natural land and water resources, of the level of agricultural technology, and of the rapid rate of population growth.

Much of the philosophical basis of the Revolution was a doctrine of nationalism that was tied to *indigenismo* ("Indianism"), an ideology which based national identity on Indian as opposed to European heritage. One aspect of Indianism is represented by the murals of Diego Rivera, which glorify the Indians and ridicule the Spaniards and their descendants who ruled the haciendas and the mines. Another embodiment is the new Museum of Anthropology in Mexico City, opened in 1964. The people of Mexico and anthropologists of many nations are justly proud of it, and even some non-Mexicans and nonanthropologists consider it to be one of the most impressive museums in the world.

Literacy, free public education, and intellectual freedom were also goals of the Revolution. Beginning in the 1920's, there were extensive efforts to improve and extend the educational system, particularly in rural areas. These efforts have continued, and today more money than ever is invested in education. Of all the Latin American countries, only Costa Rica spends a higher proportion of its national budget on schools (Cumberland 1968:322).

In the economic realm, the initial concern was agriculture, a concern that lasted through the presidency of Cárdenas. Thereafter, the big push was industrialization, and it produced what Mexicans like to call *el milagro Méxicano* ("the Mexican miracle"), rapid and sustained economic development. For three decades the annual rate of economic growth has exceeded six percent, a record that surpasses all other Latin American countries; it also surpasses the performance of the United States' economy in recent years. The "miracle" has been achieved by a mixed economy which combines public and private ownership. The government owns the oil and electric power industries, the railroads, and part or all of some manufacturing firms. Even so, the bulk of industry is in private hands, and for two decades there has been a resurgence of foreign investment.

The Revolution has transformed Mexican society in some ways, but it has not closed the gap between the rich and the poor. Programs associated with the first of its concerns, land reform, eliminated the ostentatious wealth of the great landowners; but they were unable to create a secure economy for the rapidly growing rural population. The later concern of the Revolution, the big push for industrialization, has created a new basis for distinctions of wealth. The entrepreneurs, the managers, the technicians, and the skilled industrial workers have flourished; yet they and their families constitute a small minority of the population. Most of the people in agriculture, and many urban people employed as unskilled laborers or service workers, still lead a hard, poor existence compared to that segment of the population which has benefited from economic growth. The sort of life described by Oscar Lewis in *The Children of Sanchez* (1961), although not the mode in urban Mexico, is not uncommon.

The region that forms the subject of this book has been a microcosm of the Revolution, with its chaos, its problems, and its hopes. This chapter will conclude with a discussion of the hacienda system and the earlier stages of the Revolution in the Valley of Los Llanos.

The Pulque *Haciendas*

The great landed estates of Mexico were distributed throughout various parts of the country, and their production was specialized according to region and climate. Most of the earliest haciendas were devoted to raising cattle to satisfy the demand for meat by the growing Creole and *mestizo* (mixed blood) populations of colonial times. The Plains of Los Llanos were a prime area for cattle, and some large estates developed in the region. As the herds multiplied rapidly after 1540, they overran much of the agricultural land of the Indian villages. The situation worsened to the point where the Viceroy ordered the cattlemen to clear their herds from the region. With this governmental support, the Indians drove out 10,000 head, in the face of the cattlemen's protests (Chevalier 1963:100).

In the long run, economic changes were more a function of the market than of royal policy. During colonial times the region came to specialize more and more in the production of *pulque*. It was an important drink to the Aztecs and their predecessors, and it is still the traditional beverage of the peasant and the urban working class. Plate 3 captures the delight that *pulque* still gives to those who savor it. That delight lies partly in the fact that it is the one beverage that is uniquely Mexican. Factory personnel who have warmly embraced modern ideology continue to value *pulque* as the characteristic drink of the region; (they serve it to guests, especially visiting anthropologists, as in Plate 4). Occasionally the society pages of the Mexico City newspapers report that *pulque* was consumed at fashionable parties where "typical foods" were served. These examples show that *pulque* is still appreciated. It is valued more and more as a symbol, however, not used as an everyday drink.

This "cactus beer" is still made by a simple and ancient technology. The *maguey* is a handsome plant consisting of long spikes which grow from a heart at the level of the ground; the overall height might reach nine or ten feet. A mature plant is pictured in Plate 5. The *maguey* requires at least seven years to mature, after which the heart is scraped out to form a basin in which the sap collects. Twice a day it is removed by a worker called a *tlachiquero* ("tapper"), who inserts a long, hollow gourd and sucks the sap into it. Under good conditions a plant will produce three gallons a day for three months before it dies. John Poggie (1968:30) reports that local people perceive the *maguey* as a:

> . . . bank . . . a place you can go to daily and get a little bit out. It's not like a crop which either fails or survives in only one chance per year.

The tapper carries the sap to the *tinacal* ("fermentation room") in two wooden casks mounted on either side of a donkey. It is placed in a vat with a little high-quality *pulque* to start the fermentation (see Plate 6). It ferments so rapidly that it appears to be boiling and it builds up a high head of foam. In about 24 hours, the slightly sweet, delicately flavored sap is converted into a thick, milky, strong-flavored liquid. The odor given off is even more powerful than the flavor: I have seen people unaccustomed to it run quickly from the fermentation room in order to preserve the equilibrium of their stomachs. Both the taste and the smell must be experienced to be believed.

Pulque will keep for only a day or two before turning sour. It can be canned, but the connoiseur, peasant or not, disdains the preserved product. Even today, and certainly before modern processing, the industry requires a nearby market.

That market, of course, was and is furnished primarily by Mexico City. As that metropolis grew, *pulque* became increasingly popular, and the annual consumption reached the astounding figure of 363 quarts per capita by 1916, the high point of consumption (Loyola Montemayor 1956:194). Such a large and growing market furnished a superb economic base for

Plate 3.   The pleasures of *pulque*

Plate 4.   John Poggie, Frank Miller, and friends drinking a toast
(photo by Erika Poggie)

Plate 5. The *maguey*, source of *pulque*

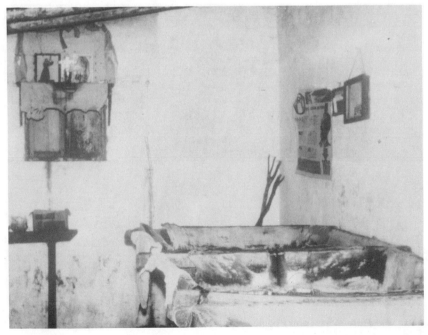

Plate 6. Fermentation vats for *pulque*

Plate 7.   The main house of an ex-hacienda

Plate 8.   Houses of agricultural workers

some of the grandest haciendas in all Mexico. They became well established by 1800, and they flourished as the population of the capital city grew from 120,000 in that year to 400,000 by the beginning of the Revolution in 1910. The *pulque* estates required large quantities of land and labor, but very little capital equipment. They took over all the productive land in the Plains of Los Llanos, and enlisted as workers the Indian and mixed-blood peasants who had previously owned it. Unlike the hacienda owners of colonial times, who were reconciled to chronic depression, the *pulque* producers had the advantage of a constantly expanding market. Making good use of the opportunity, they acquired ever larger labor forces, built fine houses on the country estates, and lived in style, usually in Mexico City. Plate 7 shows the main house, now partially empty, of one of the largest estates in the Valley of Los Llanos. The owners of the *pulque* haciendas exercised unchallenged economic and political control over the Valley of Los Llanos and over similar regions in adjacent states.

In these areas at least three-fourths of the adult males were *peones,* landless laborers working on the haciendas for extremely low wages. An important social type, they have given us an English word, peon, for a person assigned to drudgery. As we have noted, the wages were frequently paid, not in cash, but as credit at the hacienda store, where the workers bought the few necessities that their meager earnings afforded them. Many peons continued to live in their natal villages. Others who lived on the estates fared slightly better, since they were sometimes given the use of a small plot of land to raise some of their own food. Although the peons were a deprived and oppressed majority and might have seemed ripe for rebellion, the Valley of Los Llanos was not one of the springboards of the Revolution. When it came, however, the effects were broad and deep.

Effects of the Revolution

During the years of active fighting, revolutionary armies passed through the Valley; haciendas were looted and their owners forced to flee. In 1918, after the fighting had ended, the first *ejidos* were formed. The Decree of 1915 had provided that communities could recover hacienda land if they could prove that their lands had been seized illegally. Under this provision two villages near Cerro Grande formed agrarian units. But most communities in the region could not document conclusive proof, and the owners of the estates continued to resist expropriation. The rest of the *ejidos* were not formed until the 1930's, when the national government began to apply more vigorously the provision of the 1917 Constitution for outright grants of land. Eventually all but one of the villages in the network acquired communal land.

As in the rest of the nation, the land reform accomplished the important social goal of returning the land to those who worked it, but it did not succeed in solving the economic problems of the countryside. Those problems worsened because of the continuing decline of the *pulque* industry. What happened to that industry has been nicely analyzed by Charles Mundale (1917:29-40), and I shall follow his account here. Before the Revolution, the larger haciendas had their own retail outlets in Mexico City, so there was a kind of regional identification of *pulque* saloons. Quality control and brand names were lacking, but at least it was possible to know where one's daily portion came from. The most important *pulque*-producing family had its saloon on Avenida Juárez, the principal commercial street in the capital city.

The breaking up of the haciendas did not mean that they disappeared entirely. A few were abandoned; the rest continued to operate with the legal maximum of 200 hectares (494 acres), or a larger amount in the names of various relatives. The fermentation room processed the sap gathered from the cactus on this land by a few wage laborers. It also processed sap sold to it by the former peons, who now had their own parcels of land, where they collected sap as independent operators.

Those parcels of land were now the only means of survival for the tappers; they no longer had the security, minimal as it had been, of association with a great estate. Consequently they over-exploited their resources: they tapped the cactus too young, and did not always show much diligence in planting new ones, which after all would not start producing for at least seven years.

The process of fermentation requires hardly more capital

investment than the collection of sap; as the number of independent tappers skyrocketed, the number of small breweries proliferated, and the identification of *pulque* with its hacienda source largely disappeared. The opportunities for adulteration also expanded, and some saloons augmented the volume by as much as a hundred percent.

The image of the product, although long-established and well-revered, proved increasingly incongruous as Mexico became more modernized. It was, and is, the beverage *par excellence* of the peasant and the urban proletariat. Yet, the unsanitary conditions of production and distribution are well known, and, appropriately, there has never been any advertising of the product. Few contemporary producers are large enough to afford advertising, and there is no association to sponsor billboards proclaiming "Everybody needs *pulque*."

The "image problem" and the changes in production and distribution contributed to a switch in public taste that no doubt would have happened anyway as the nation modernized: the consumption of beer rose rapidly as the popularity of *pulque* fell. In Mexico City, the annual per capita consumption of the cactus beer declined from the high point of 363 quarts in 1916 to 61 in 1953. Nationwide, the decline was from 23 to 15 quarts between 1943 and 1953, while beer consumption rose from 13 to 21 (Loyola Montemayor 1956:191-94). In the new Mexico the beverage of the common man is beer. *Pulque* is identified with the past; and the industry which produces it is inefficient and obsolete.

Adaptive Strategies in Agriculture

The economic and social structures brought into being by the Revolution created a new environment in which individuals had to operate and to which they had to adapt if they were to survive. Two kinds of strategies emerged: *pulque* production on a vastly smaller scale than formerly in the haciendas; and a new concentration on the production of barley.

The mode of adjustment to new conditions varied according to the nature of the social unit. Most of the estates, now quaintly called ex-haciendas, continued to operate, but did so on a greatly reduced scale. One that I visited several times holds the legal maximum of 200 hectares (494 acres) of land. It is owned by a small group of businessmen which includes relatives of the owner in the days before the land reform. The manager from those days still serves; he shows neither his years nor the travail of a major revolution. This estate has always been relatively small; the main house is only one story, and generally modest by hacienda standards. The former owner lived in Mexico City and used the estate as a country home. Now the owners visit only on special occasions, and most of the establishment is somewhat down at the heels. The stately furniture is still in the sitting room, but the roof leaks and the floor is rotting. The manager and his wife occupy the simpler living quarters to the rear. Their nondescript upholstered chairs and shiny stereo console seem out of place beside the slightly musty walls.

This ex-hacienda employs only seven full-time workers to collect *maguey* sap and to plant some corn and barley. They live about a mile away in the village where all the peons used to live, and which is now an *ejido* formed of the bulk of the estate's former lands. Their relationship to the manager seems still to be what it once was—ready obedience and deference. Unlike earlier times, they are free to seek work elsewhere, but their mobility is limited by lack of skills and by the ties of locality and kinship.

The brewery where the *pulque* is fermented is one large room with five vats. The product is shipped by truck to Mexico City in the traditional wooden casks. Forty years ago, when the output was many times what it is today, it went directly by train along the tracks nearby.

Many ex-haciendas operate in this way, although often on a somewhat larger scale. They tend to be on the hilly flanks of the valley, where the terrain is suitable only for *maguey*. Of those few that were once on the valley floor, most have been abandoned or at least no longer produce *pulque*. The good valley bottom land has been taken over almost entirely by *ejidos* devoted to the production of barley.

The pulque industry was already stagnant when the *ejidos* were formed during the 1930's. The new landholders began to discover some elementary principles. For all the abuses inherent in the hacienda system, it had involved what economists call economics of scale; that is, the efficiencies of large-scale operations. A large labor force working a large area to supply one large brewery was more efficient than a collection of individual operators tapping their own small expanses of *maguey* for several small breweries. The inefficiencies of small units has been a general problem of the *ejido* system, and they have been especially evident in the *pulque* business.

This was one lesson of economics; the other was the changing nature of the market. As the taste for beer spread, the demand for barley went up. Small quantities of this crop had been grown for centuries in the region; but beginning in the 1940's, the *ejidos* with good valley land planted more and more barley, and today it is their principal product. Each adult male member has use rights to a plot of land which he works himself, sometimes with the help of relatives or hired hands. In most *ejidos* the heavy work of plowing and weeding is done by one or more men who own tractors; they are the capitalists in a system of communal landholding.

Growing barley to make a living is subject to serious constraints. The climate is a major problem. In an area where the rainfall is so unreliable, growing crops is a risky way to make a living. The crop was severely reduced by drought in 1967, and it failed again in 1969. The scarcity of flat land in the valley is another constraint. Even in a year of adequate rainfall, the available land can support only a limited number of people. Small-scale irrigation, improved seed, and better technology could expand the agricultural potential of the area; but its meager natural endowments impose limits that no amount of human effort or ingenuity can overcome.

CHAPTER THREE

Images of the
"Mexican Village"

The Mexican village is the creation of anthropologists. By that I mean that North Americans' conceptions about communities south of the Rio Grande have been created, not by residents of those communities, but by social scientists who have sojourned in them from time to time.

In the United States, there are two sorts of images of the Mexican village. People who have traveled to Mexico have seen for themselves the dry fields, the dusty streets, the relaxed but friendly pace of life, the simple homes, and the poverty. They tend to assume, probably unconsciously, the Calvinist view that poverty signifies a lack of grace, which equals a kind of inferiority.

Those who have read or studied some anthropology have a more elaborate image, to which a number of classic community studies have contributed. Robert Redfield (1930) began a fine tradition of anthropological research with his study of Tepoztlán, a village about 50 miles southwest of Mexico City. A restudy by Oscar Lewis (1951) kindled a famous controversy. Although they agreed on many things, Redfield presented a somewhat idyllic picture of the village, and Lewis questioned that view with data about interpersonal conflict and hostility. Still, there is a unity within the diversity of these and other views, a unity that has been captured best in Eric Wolf's (1955, 1957) concept of the "closed corporate community."

The Closed Corporate Community. This concept highlights the inter-relationships of the structural features of a certain type of peasant village in Mexico, in other countries of Latin America, and elsewhere in the world.

A closed corporate peasant community exists on marginal land under communal control: the land is usually owned in common, occasionally owned individually, and in each case sometimes carries taboos against selling or renting to outsiders. The land, worked with a traditional technology, yields a low level of income. In other words, the community is poor. Any further economic burden, such as population growth or the imposition of taxes, requires a "compensatory economic reaction in the field of production," such as wage labor, the sale of crafts, or other means. The basic economic unit is the nuclear family. As a producing unit, it does not carry on any cost-accounting of its inputs of labor, and therefore can increase the performance of unpaid work. As a consuming unit, it can readily cut expenditures to a bare subsistence level.

Virtually all Latin American peasants are Catholics. The religion of the Indian peasants is "folk-Catholicism," a combination of European and Indian religious features which is itself an integrated system of belief and practice. This system is tied to the formal political organization of the village, forming what anthropologists have called the "civil-religious hierarchy." It is so named because it is a system of ranked roles through which office-holders move during periodic terms over the years.

The members of the community see the civil-religious hierarchy as a single system. They also recognize that it has two aspects—one concerned with secular affairs and the other with religious matters—but they do not make nearly as sharp a distinction between the two as do most North Americans. The system as a whole is both the principal means for defining the community boundaries and the main symbol of the entity to which the members give their primary allegiance. The community, organized around the civil-religious hierarchy, is the unit which gives the individual his cultural identity. Beyond that, the extent to which he recognizes citizenship in the Mexican nation varies considerably, depending on the community's degree of isolation, the availability of education, and other, similar factors.

The solidarity of the community is acted out several times a year in the fiestas that honor the patron saint and other saints represented by images in the church. These fiestas are engaging combinations of solemn ritual and happy celebration, with feasting, drinking, and fireworks. The people gather to reaffirm their devotion to the saints and their commitment to each other and to their community.

The system also operates among its members as an economic leveling mechanism. The main avenue to prestige is to hold a series of increasingly responsible offices over a period of years. The higher religious offices are devoted to sponsorship of the annual round of fiestas, and the office-holders are obligated personally to finance much of their considerable expense. The cost to an individual might be four or five times his annual cash income. The wealthier members are expected to hold these offices, and when they do, they have to sell their resources (such as horses and cattle) and sometimes go into debt in order to raise enough money. In a sense, the small economic surplus is invested back into the community, in the form of support for activities which symbolize collective unity.

Fiestas are not the only leveling mechanism. They are paralleled by what Wolf (1955:460) calls "institutionalized envy": a culturally defined tendency to envy those with wealth, power, or privilege that is notably above average. Since envy is thought to cause illness in those who are its object, fear of this envy operates as a brake on the acquisition of wealth or power and on the acceptance of innovations from the wider society.

Wolf (1955:459) defines two other cultural orientations which characterize the closed corporate community: "defensive ignorance, an active denial of outside alternatives which, if accepted, might threaten the corporate structure"; and a "cult of poverty" which extolls the virtue of hard work and the merits of the simple life.

One of the merits of Wolf's analysis is that he shows the interrelationships among economic, structural, and ideological elements, which combine to isolate the community and defend it against outside influences. His model applies best to those Indian groups with a strong and distinctive cultural identity which has been preserved through four centuries of vicissitudes, first at the hands of the Spanish conquerors, then from the Creole colonialists, and finally from Mexican nationalists. Those Indian groups are a small minority of the population, but because they have been the focus of anthropological interest, they have also been the source of North American images of the Mexican village.

I have discussed at some length the features of the closed corporate community in order to set up a contrast with the towns and villages in the Valley of Los Llanos. They are relatively open and not characterized by collective defense against outside influences. To be sure, they are only relatively open: most land is *ejido* land and is therefore restricted to use by members of the community. The nuclear family is the most important social unit, but not the basic economic unit as it is in systems of subsistence agriculture. In this area, people involved in farming are either raising cash crops on their *ejido* plots or working for someone who does. Many people are not farmers at all, but instead are merchants or factory workers. The civil-religious hierarchy and the fiesta system do not exist in the form familiar to many anthropologists. Community participation in religious life is likely to involve little more than attending mass or going on organized pilgrimages to the shrine of the Virgin of Guadalupe, the patron saint of Mexico, in the outskirts of Mexico City.

Although some local residents are rustic by urban standards, there is little of what Wolf called "defensive ignorance." On the contrary, there is an eagerness for knowledge of the wider world and a commitment to—really an excessive faith in—education as the means to individual advancement and general human betterment.

The Image of Limited Good. The concept of the closed corporate community is a set of ideas about how people have organized themselves to resist change and to maintain their identity. Another view of resistance to change in traditional Mexican villages emphasizes ideological factors. On the basis of research spanning twenty years in Tzintzuntzan on the shores of Lake Pátzcuaro, George Foster has argued that the behavior of the villagers can be understood best in the light of a model which he calls the "image of limited good." This model states that the members of the community see their world as one in which all valued things—wealth, health, love, honor, power, safety, etc.—*"exist in absolute quantities insufficient to fill even minimal needs of villagers"* (Foster 1967:123; his italics). In addition, they are convinced that there is no direct action they can take to increase the available supplies.

In elaborating the model, Foster states that it is methodologically useful to make an assumption that is actually contrary to fact, and to treat Tzintzuntzan as if it existed in a vacuum, entirely closed off from the wider society. He argues that to do so is simply to accept the assumption of the Tzintzuntzeño, whose perception of natural and social resources is limited to the immediate area. If this assumption is accepted and if the system is viewed as closed, then it follows that *"an individual or a family can improve its position only at the expense of others"* (Foster 1967:124; his italics).

The fundamental question that can be raised about Foster's approach concerns the direction of the relationship between ideology and behavior. This is an ancient problem in intellectual history, and one that has not been resolved by either anthropology or the other social sciences. Foster uses his model to explain a wide spectrum of behavior ranging from economics to friendship to tales of treasure. In doing so he seems to assume that the "image of limited good" is a basic cause of a range of behaviors, including a strong tendency to resist change. I am inclined to view the ideology as an effect as well as a cause: that is, as an adaptation to a set of circumstances. The circumstances are an economy of scarcity, and the "image of limited good" justifies and rationalizes the way things are. The implication of this view is that the ideology is capable of changing rapidly when modern technology demonstrates that the supply of some of the good things of life is not severely limited, but instead is rapidly expandable. In fact, I shall argue that this change of ideology is now taking place in the area surrounding the new town.

There is another point about the anthropological image of the Mexican village that needs to be made emphatically, and that is, that the image is shaped, not only by the kinds of analysis carried out by anthropologists, but also by the selection of research sites. The communities studied have tended to be relatively traditional places where the Indian heritage is still strong, and Foster and Wolf have given good accounts of these kinds of communities. Nevertheless, they are certainly not typical of the thousands of Mexican villages, most of which are not Indian and many of which are changing rapidly. I do not claim that the Valley of Los Llanos is a typical region, but I do claim that its villages represent a type that have been neglected in anthropological research. They are neither scenic nor exotic; the Indian heritage has been greatly diluted; and the few crafts that exist are crude compared to crafts in other areas of the country. But these villages represent the conditions of life for a great number of rural Mexicans, and their growing commitment to modernization seems to be, for good or for ill, the wave of the future.

CHAPTER FOUR

The Network of Villages

The pattern of human settlement in the Valley of Los Llanos is typical of Mexico. Most people live in towns, villages, and hamlets; few occupy the kind of isolated farmstead that is characteristic of rural parts of the United States. Most farmers do not reside on their farmland but instead live in settlements, however small, and go out to the fields to work. Similarly, the animals are kept in the compound or near the house at night, and taken out to pasture during the day.

The pattern of daily activity is that men go away to work, whether in the fields, in the factories, or at some other occupation. Most women are in or around the house during most of the day. When they go out, it is to go to market, to visit relatives or to gather at the local fountain or laundry tubs to wash clothes and to socialize. These days most children between the ages of six and twelve are in school, so they are also gone during the day. Evening is a time for social interaction, though it is almost always segregated: women chat in doorways, men gather on street corners, and children play in the streets.

The Distribution of Population

The concentration of people in villages is rather striking in the Valley of Los Llanos. Table 4.1 shows that 60 percent of the communities have fewer than 500 people, and almost 90 percent have fewer than 2,000.

Table 4.1. Size of Communities

Population Range	Number of Communities	Cumulative Percentage
45 – 99	6	12.0%
100 – 499	24	60.0%
500 – 999	11	82.0%
1000 – 1999	3	88.0%
2000 – 2999	0	88.0%
3000 and over	6	100.0%

In fact, two of the three villages in the range 1,000-1,999 have only slightly more than 1,000 people. The six places over 3,000 are the town centers and the new town.

In any society it is difficult to draw a line between "towns" and "villages," since the terms do not denote measurable differences. In this area of Mexico, I would say that the town centers and the new town can be called "towns," not only because of their size but also because of their functions and their places in the political structure. The populations of the other communities are all under 2,000 and can be considered "villages," although in a more sparsely populated part of the country a community of 1,500 would offer more services and might be considered a town. Table 4.1 does not include the rare isolated farmsteads: there are only four, all in the *municipio* of Malapan.

Individual communities are the most visible social units in the area: no matter how small, each has a name and, with few exceptions, a line devoted to it in the national census. Each has a physical structure: a variety of buildings arranged along streets and paths. But there is an additional level of social reality which cannot be perceived with the naked eye, partly because its physical scope is too large and partly because its essence is the nature of the relationship among its constituent units. That additional reality is the network formed by the towns, villages, and hamlets in the Valley.

The Network

Just as individuals group together to form communities, communities group to form a higher-order entity that I am calling a network. The concept has two facets: it involves both a set of communities and the sum total of social bonds by which they are joined. In the abstract it would be possible to imagine what the sum total would be: the relationships between buyers and sellers, the ties of kinship and friendship, the connections among schools, the rivalries among the athletic teams, and all of the other contacts that make up human social life. For our research, it is not necessary to describe all the ties that compose the network; but it is useful to delineate its extent by determining which communities are included and which are not. This part of the project was carried out by John Poggie in 1966, and the method that he used was originally used by Frank and Ruth Young in their research on the region during 1957-58. They defined the network by interviewing the person who occupied the top political position in each community, and by asking him a simple question: "With what other villages around here does this one have the most contact?" In other words, they defined the network in terms of the perceptions of key informants, not in terms of their own observation of actual contact.

Poggie defined the network in the same manner so that his results would be comparable to those that the Youngs obtained eight years earlier, particularly since all other evidence confirms that the perceptions of key informants represent patterns of actual contact. This research strategy proved to be eminently worthwhile because it revealed considerable change in the configuration of the network between 1958 and 1966. At both times the general pattern was that villages had the most contact with the town center of their *municipio*. In 1958, Los Llanos was the hub of the network in terms of social, commercial and cultural contact if not in terms of physical space: it was chosen by two of the town centers (Cerro Grande and Benito Juárez), Ciudad Industrial, and four villages as the place with which they had the most contact (Young 1964:37). Cerro Grande was almost as central: it was chosen by two town centers (Los Llanos and Malapan) and four villages. At that time, three years after the factories began operating, Ciudad Industrial was no more important, in terms of contact choices, than a number of villages: it was chosen only by Cristóbal, a nearby community into which growing numbers of factory workers were moving.

By 1966 the new town had become the hub of the network: it was chosen by three town centers and three villages (Poggie 1968:59). Los Llanos was still the commercial center of the region, but it now took a secondary place in the network, being chosen by five places. Cerro Grande had dropped to third place with only four choices.

The movement of Ciudad Industrial into a position of social and commercial centrality is hardly surprising. Both during and after its construction, it rapidly became the main source of non-agricultural employment, and some of the wage levels have been lucrative by local standards. Its population has grown to be almost as large as that of Los Llanos: 12,327 as compared to 13,705 in the 1970 census. During the same period Los Llanos has nevertheless maintained its role as the market center and commercial leader of the Valley. The new town's rise to prominence has affected the interrelationships among communities in the network, but it has not altered them drastically.

Institutional Complexity

Another changing trend has been the development of communities in the direction of greater complexity, with the addition of new facilities, services, organizations, and social roles. In our research we wanted a systematic way to compare communities with respect to this dimension. Again we followed the lead of Frank and Ruth Young, who had "measured" complexity by the scaling technique developed by Louis Guttman (1944).

A Guttman scale is a little like a spelling test in which the participants are asked to spell words of increasing difficulty. Suppose Jim, John, and Joe are asked to spell "cat," "cattle," and "catastrophe." Suppose, also, that the test yields the results represented in Table 4.2, which is arranged in a format called a "scalogram," with an "X" for each word spelled correctly. The special characteristic of a Guttman scale is that both the units of observation (Jim, etc.) and the items ("cat," etc.) are ranked, the former from best to worst performer, the latter from easiest to hardest. It follows that we can predict performance on all other items if we know only the number that an individual got right. If we know that Joe got only one word right, we can predict that it was "cat." Therefore, the "Scale Step" indicates not only how many were right, but which ones were right. Thus a Guttman scale is a technique for discovering two kinds of order in the phenomena being investigated: it ranks both the units of observation and the items which define the scale. This important point can be illustrated further by the scalogram of institutional complexity in Table 4.3.

Table 4.2. Scalogram of a Simple Spelling Test

Units of Observation	"Cat"	"Cattle"	"Catastrophe"	Scale Step
Jim	X	X	X	3
John	X	X		2
Joe	X			1

When John Poggie conducted the survey of key informants in 1966, he used the same interview schedule that the Youngs had used eight years before. The interview covered, among other things, a considerable amount of information about facilities, organizations, and social roles in each community. From this information, fourteen items were selected to define institutional complexity; these items are listed across the top of the scalogram. The twenty-two communities studied in the network are listed down the left side, where I have given names only for those discussed in this book. There is a column for each of the items, and an "X" indicates when the item is present. The least complex community, at the bottom of the scalogram, has none of the features except a name. The two most complex, at the top, have all the features.

Table 4.3. Scalogram of Institutional Complexity, 1966

Scale Items

1. Named, autonomous community
2. Church
3. One or more organizations
4. One or more officials
5. School building
6. Functioning school
7. Access to railroad
8. Electricity
9. Railroad station
10. Six grades in school
11. Public square
12. One or more telephones
13. Doctor
14. Secondary school

	Community	1	2	3	4	5	6	7	8	9	10	11	12	13	14	Scale Steps
1.	Los Llanos	X	X	X	X	X	X	X	X	X	X	X	X	X	X	10
2.			X	X	X	X	X	X	X	X	X	X	X	X	X	
3.	Benito Juárez	X	X	X	X	X	X	X	X	X	X	X	X	X		9
4.	Malapan	X	X	X	X	X	X	X	X	X	X	X	X	X		
5.	Cerro Grande	X	X	X	X	X	X	X	X	O	X	X	X	X		♦
6.			X	X	X	X	X	X	X	X	X	X	O	X		8
7.			X	X	X	X	X	X	X	X	X	O	X			
8.			X	X	X	X	X	X	X	X	X	X	X			7
9.	Adonde		X	X	X	X	X	X	X	X	X	O	X			
10.	Cristóbal	X	X	X	X	X	X	X	X	X						6
11.		X	X	X	X	X	X	X	X	X						
12.	Rocavista	X	X	X	X	X	X	X	X							5
13.		X	X	X	X	X	X	X	X							
14.	Santa Cecilia	X	X	X	X	X	X	X								4
15.		X	X	X	X	X	X	X								
16.	San Manuel	X	X	X	X	X	X									3
17.		X	X	X	X	X	X									
18.		X	X	X	X	X	X									
19.		X	X	X	X	X	X									
20.		X	X	X	X											2
21.		X	X	X	X											
22.		X														1

Coefficient of reproducibility = .99
Coefficient of scalability = .93

The simplified example of the spelling test formed a "perfect" scale in the sense that every person who could spell a difficult word could also spell all the easier words. However, this scale of complexity is not perfect, because four O's appear where we would expect X's. These absences of expected items are called "scale errors" because they are failures of predictability; this simply means that there are some irregularities among the regularities of social life. The occurrences of the irregularities would surprise few observers of the human scene; what *is* surprising is the high degree of order revealed by the scale. The coefficients of reproducibility and of scalability are measures of reliability: both are very high, indicating that the scale is a reliable tool for studying institutional complexity (see Guttman 1944 and Menzel 1953).

Although the scalogram summarizes much information about the communities, thus making verbal descriptions unnecessary, a few points are worth emphasizing. The scalogram can be read in either direction. Reading across each row gives the scale items found in each community: for example, No. 16, San Manuel, has items 1 through 6. Reading down each column shows which communities have each scale item: for example, only the top five communities have item 12, telephone service.

The scale encompasses the nineteen largest settlements in the network (all over 500 in population), but does not include the new town. It also includes three smaller places that are centrally located. The other twenty-seven settlements had, as of 1966, none of the fourteen defining features except a name: no organizations, no schools, no electricity, and no doctors. As a matter of fact, many of the communities in the scalogram did not have these items either: only thirteen had electricity, only seven had full primary schools of six grades, and only five had doctors.

The information in the scalogram is useful, not only for comparing communities at the present time, but also for studying trends of change. Some of these trends have been affected, directly or indirectly, by the presence of Ciudad Industrial. The discussion of most aspects of the regional impact of that project will be reserved until later in this book; but some of the changes will be discussed in the next chapter, as part of the description of the character of individual communities. A more complete account of the use of Guttman scales for studying change may be found in Poggie and Miller (1969).

CHAPTER FIVE

The Character of Communities

Our emphasis on the concept of the network in our discussion of the Valley of Los Llanos is a result of our interest in treating the region as an entity in its own right. We have also emphasized the need to gather systematic data for comparing communities; the Guttman scale of institutional complexity has served this purpose. But we are also committed to the more traditional anthropological interest in understanding the character of individual communities, and this commitment raises the question of selecting locales for further study.

In Chapter 3, I argued that the anthropological image of the Mexican village is shaped by the selection of research sites as well as by the assumptions and strategies used in analyzing data. I would argue further that anthropology as a discipline is naive about the problem of sampling. Many anthropologists seem to assume that an intensive study of a single community over the course of a full year yields such vast and diverse quantities of information that sampling is not a problem. From the perspective of that particular community, they may be right. But the selection of that community in the first place is an act of sampling. Decisions about research sites are sometimes, perhaps even frequently, made on the basis of non-scientific criteria. A certain place may be the most scenic or appear the most interesting, or it may be the community to which the anthropologist can most readily gain access.

The issue is important, partly because no matter how much an anthropologist may warn against generalizing results from one village to an entire region or nation, the wider public audience for anthropological writings will do just that. No one knows for sure what students and ex-students of the discipline think about Mexico, but I suspect that their images are shaped by books on a narrow range of villages that do not represent that nation's dynamism and diversity.

In planning our research in Mexico, we devised a strategy for attempting to resolve these kinds of issues. For the survey of households, we wanted to include locales that were representative of the economic and social variation in the region, and we wanted to base the choice on systematic data that were comparable across communities. We also wanted to maximize the possibilities of using the Youngs' data as a baseline for studying change.

While in the field, John Poggie analyzed some of the data from the survey of key informants and constructed a preliminary version of the scale of institutional complexity. His work gave us a firm empirical basis for making decisions about the sample to be included in the survey of households. In order to maximize the possibilities for comparisons over time, we quickly decided on the four communities that the Youngs had included in their survey: Cerro Grande, Benito Juárez, Cristóbal, and Rocavista. Their original choices had been fortunate, because these places represent a great deal of the diversity in the region and furnish some intriguing contrasts. Cerro Grande, for example, is long-established; in fact, it is the oldest settlement in the Valley. Benito Juárez, on the other hand, is one of the newer. It was founded in 1932, when it acquired *ejido* land as part of the land reform of the Revolution. The former town appears seasoned and venerable, the latter raw and new. Both include many factory workers and other people engaged in non-agricultural occupations.

Cristóbal and Rocavista are both villages in the *municipio* of Cerro Grande, equidistant from the highway and from the new town. The former has a significant number of men employed in industry, the latter almost none. Both have most of their land on the level bottom of the valley, and consequently neither produces much *pulque*.

In order to broaden the range of variation represented, we included three other villages in the survey. They are all predominantly agricultural and are farther from the new town than the four places discussed above. Santa Cecilia, in the *municipio* of Benito Juárez, is close to its town center but less accessible because it is on a dirt road. Adonde lies along the southern edge of the network, in the *municipio* of Los Llanos. San Manuel is located in the far northeastern corner and is the least accessible because it lies on a poor dirt road that is impassible during parts of the rainy season.

Each of the seven communities has a character of its own derived from its location, its history, and the composition of its population.

Cerro Grande. On the lower slopes of the small mountain in the middle of the Valley of Los Llanos, Cerro Grande lies in the shadows of its fine colonial church, whose venerable dome of bright yellow tile is visible for miles. The church reveals the importance of the town during the colonial era, and the fact that it was constructed on the site of a pyramid symbolizes one of the great transitions in Mexico's history. A nearby pyramid has been partially excavated by archaeologists, and shows the relationship the region had to Teotihuacán during pre-Columbian times.

Of all the places in the Valley, Cerro Grande is the most like a traditional Mexican town. The church overlooks the central plaza, whose atypical design is overshadowed by its characteristic function as the center of activity. The highway threads through town on narrow streets around the plaza, which is usual; but the plaza itself is merely a wide median strip between the streets, not a standard square. Even so, it is lined with shops, small restaurants, saloons, and the town hall; and the permanent market lies on the down-hill side. Perhaps the most complimentary thing that could be said about the plaza is that it is unpretentious. Since the region is dry, the trees are few and rather straggly, offering scant shade for the concrete benches which are decorated by plaques bearing the names of the donors. There are no flowers: any that might be crowded in would probably be trampled.

These unenthusiastic remarks about the plaze belie the sense of well-being that can be attained by sitting under the arcade of the old buildings, sipping a glass of superb Mexican beer on a hot spring afternoon—the warmest of the year in highland Mexico, where the summer is cooled by the rains—and chatting about the state of the market for *pulque* and the relative merits of Renaults and Volkswagens.

The highways through town are paved with concrete or asphalt; the other central streets are cobblestone; and some of the outlying streets are dirt. Since the town lies on a slope with some steep inclines, the streets also serve as sluiceways for summer storms, and are therefore more likely to be impassable to automobiles than those in nearby communities. Few residents own automobiles, so that sort of traffic is light; but the steady stream of buses and trucks is impressive, though disconcerting to those enjoying the plaza.

At the north end of the plaza and also up the street are ancient "fountains" in which water trickles over carved spouts into basins. The compose the central water system, built shortly after the Spanish Conquest, and the water is supplied by an aqueduct running sixteen miles to the mountains in the east.

Cerro Grande has experienced a spectacular growth of population since the coming of the new town. Table 5.1 summarizes information on populations and occupations in the communities included in the survey of households. Cerro

Table 5.1. Population and Occupations In
Communities in the Survey

Community	Population			Percentages of Occupations in the Work Force, 1967		
	1950	1970	Percentage of Growth	Farmer	Factory Worker	Other
Cerro Grande	1330	7027	428.3%	23.2%	31.3%	45.5%
Benito Juárez	1781	3874	117.5%	44.0%	22.7%	33.3%
Cristóbal	356	788	121.3%	44.3%	38.1%	17.6%
Rocavista	321	418	30.2%	80.0%	9.4%	10.6%
Santa Cecilia	446	569	27.6%	78.4%	8.8%	12.8%
Adonde	1279	1744	36.4%	72.1%	14.4%	13.5%
San Manuel	524	571	9.0%	94.2%	None	5.8%

Grande's growth from 1,330 to 7,027 in twenty years is by far the greatest of any community in the region. During the same period, the size of the nation has doubled, but the size of Cerro Grande has increased more than four times. As one might expect, this change is a direct effect of Ciudad Industrial: how it has occurred will be documented later in this book.

Cerro Grande is both the largest community in the survey and the most commercial. It's distribution of occupations (see Table 3.4) is also directly attributable to the new town. In the case of factory workers, the point is obvious. The very high percentage of "other" occupations includes merchants, municipal and industrial administrative officials, professionals and technicians (such as teachers, engineers, and draftsmen), and people in diverse services, such as policemen and barbers. In a sense, there is a branch of Ciudad Industrial in Cerro Grande: a housing development on the outskirts is owned by one of the factories and the units are rented at reasonable rates to its personnel. This section of town contributes to the high percentages of factory workers and "others." In the rest of the town, not all of those in the "other" category are employed by the factories; but the livelihood of most depends directly or indirectly on those who are. The stores, second only to those in Los Llanos in number and variety, serve the entire community and surrounding territory. With the exception of a few relatively wealthy doctors and merchants, the factory employees have the most money to spend. They tend to make their major purchases—televisions, appliances, and furniture—in Mexico City; but what they spend locally is spent in Ciudad Industrial, Cerro Grande, or Los Llanos.

The low percentage of farmers in Cerro Grande does not mean that their absolute numbers are few; because it is the largest town in the survey, there are more than in any of the other communities except for Benito Juárez, and they have significant holdings of land.

Most of Cerro Grande's agricultural land is in an *ejido* of 6,200 acres. It was formed in 1930, with a nucleus of 200 original members, after the land was expropriated from several small haciendas. In 1938 and in 1943, additional land was added to provide plots for migrants and for sons of the original members. About half of the present holdings are good land in the valley bottom, where barley is the main crop, supplemented by some corn and beans. The other half of the land is on the mountain slopes and is used as pasture principally for goats and donkeys, with a few horses, cows, and sheep. The slopes are also devoted to *maguey*, which grows in three different patterns: scattered around in a semi-wild state; crowded together in hedgerows; and, on the gentler slopes, in large fields with neat rows made formidable by the tall spikes. The importance of *maguey* is demonstrated by the presence in Cerro Grande of eight *tinacales*, the fermentation plants that produce *pulque*. All of these enterprises are small, some occupying only one room. Some of the product is sold locally, but most is shipped daily by truck to Mexico City. The production of *pulque* is a full-time occupation for only a few people: the men who operate the fermentation plants, and a few men who have no other work than tapping *maguey*. But the business yields a supplementary income for both part-time tappers and those who do not tap their own plants but receive shares from those who do. *Pulque* is still a significant, if declining, agricultural endeavor.

Just as it is urban in its occupational composition, Cerro Grande is also relatively urban in institution complexity. It has all of the items in the Guttman scale except a railroad station and a secondary school. As a matter of fact, it once had a station, but it was down the hill a couple of miles from the town, and, by virtue of location, it has become the station for Ciudad Industrial.

The first primary school in Cerro Grande was founded in 1930. Another was established in 1954, and a large addition was added to the first in 1965, with financial assistance from the factories. The first year of a secondary school was also established in 1965, but the effort to develop education further was soon abandoned through lack of resources. Most of the local children who are fortunate enough to continue their schooling go to the new town, and the others go to public or private schools elsewhere.

Although Cerro Grande has grown greatly in size, it has not grown in complexity—as defined by the scale—since the Youngs' research in 1957-1958. It has acquired no new items in the scale during that period. The immediate explanation is contained in the preceding discussion: Cerro Grande had lost its railroad station and failed in the effort to develop a secondary school. A broader explanation would refer to cycles and constraints in the development of communities. By 1957 Cerro Grande had already acquired the basic facilities of a small town center. It had the older features of church and public square, and the new of electricity, telephone, and a doctor. The next step in the scale—a secondary school—represents a large investment for a Mexican town. Even so, many such schools have been built in towns the size of Cerro Grande during the past decade. No doubt Cerro Grande would also have been included but for the existence of a large high school in the new town. That project has brought great benefits, but it also imposes some limits on the development of Cerro Grande.

One of the benefits traceable to the new town has been the commercial growth we have spoken of, that has come from increased population and large payrolls. Although the town of Los Llanos traditionally has been, and still is, the commercial center of the region, merchants in Cerro Grande have proliferated and prospered with the coming of the new town. As economic development has proceeded at varying rates in different parts of Mexico, many new kinds of stores have been established. This progress has occurred more rapidly in Cerro Grande than in any other community in the Valley, with the exception of Ciudad Industrial. Since 1950 the following types of enterprises have been established (Gold 1968:45):

1. Taxi
2. Service station
3. Restaurant
4. Hotel
5. Beauty parlor
6. Newsstand
7. Metal workshop making windows and doors principally
8. Hardware and building materials store
9. Chicken and egg cooperative
10. Soft drink and beer supplier
11. Coffin maker and funeral supplier
12. Dry cleaner

The character of Cerro Grande derives from the parodoxes of its history: it is both the oldest town in the area, and the closest to Ciudad Industrial. The musty charm of its antiquity is increasingly eclipsed by the bustle of a technological society.

Benito Juárez. If Cerro Grande is a creature of the old Mexico, Benito Juárez is a creation of the new. Founded after the Revolution and shaped by the forces of land reform and industry, it appears new, unfinished, and oriented to the future. It lies on the highway about ten miles south of Ciudad Industrial, just across the railroad tracks from one of the largest former haciendas in the region. The railroad is the main line from Mexico City to the states of Puebla, Oaxaca, and Veracruz. Between the hacienda and the town is the old station from which large amounts of *pulque* were shipped to Mexico City when the hacienda was thriving before the Revolution. The railroad workers who maintained the tracks lived nearby; and it was they, rather than the peons on the estate, who took the lead in forming the *ejido* attached to the town.

In the late 1920's, some of the peons joined the railroad workers in petitioning the government for a grant of land to form an *ejido* and a community. The owner of the hacienda attempted to stave off expropriation of his land by donating 100 hectares (247 acres) for a town site to the organizing group. His generosity under pressure was insufficient to protect his interests: eventually the land was expropriated, and the *ejido* was formed in 1932 (Simon 1972).

Like most of the communities formed during the Revolution, Benito Juárez lies near an ex-hacienda; but it is unlike the others in the rapidity of its growth and development. Many of the *ejido* communities are "new towns" in the sense that they were founded only thirty years ago, but Benito Juárez is the only one that has attained both significant size and the status of a town center. It was part of the *municipio* of Cerro Grande until 1943, when it became the head town of its own *municipio*.

Although it is new, Benito Juárez is laid out in the traditional grid pattern around a central plaza, which is planted with trees, shrubs, and flowers, and is criss-crossed by tidy paths of red volcanic cinder. Facing the square are a few houses and shops, the town hall, and the school, with its outdoor basketball court. The plaza, in contrast to Cerro Grande's, is new, open, and uncrowded. Most of the small stores and shops are along the highway, which runs through town on the other side of the school. Except for the main throughfares, the streets are dirt and are dusty in the dry season and muddy in the wet.

An interesting feature of this community is the location of the church, a block away from the plaza. The building itself, still not entirely finished, jars the senses of anyone accustomed to the beautiful colonial churches of Mexico. The walls of brick and fieldstone have an interesting texture, but the squat concrete steeple that serves in place of a traditional dome seems to be an incongruous intrusion of vaguely Northern European origin.

The growth of population in Benito Juárez during the past two decades has been 117.5 percent (see Table 5.1), only slightly more than the national average, but much more than in communities of comparable size. Because Benito Juárez is young, an unusually high percentage of its inhabitants, about 80 percent, were elsewhere. Some of these people came from land-poor areas during the 1930's to take up *ejido* plots; others are factory employees who arrived after 1955; still others are merchants who came to serve the growing population.

The second largest community in the survey, Benito Juárez is also the second most "urban" as measured by the distribution of occupations. It has the second lowest percentage of farmers and the second highest "other" workers. This category includes the same kinds of people as it does in Cerro Grande, but there are fewer representatives of management, commerce, and the professions. Benito Juárez is third in the proportion of factory workers, behind Cerro Grande and Cristóbal, which is something of a "dormitory suburb" of Ciudad Industrial.

Of the communities in our sample, Benito Juárez has the largest absolute number of farmers and farm workers. The reason is simple: it has the largest amount of good land. All of the 5,000 acres in the *ejido* are valley bottom land. Barley and corn are the principal crops, but beans are also raised for both the national market and home consumption. The production of *pulque* is declining but still important: fermentation plants have decreased from six to three in recent years. Some *maguey* grows in hedgerows in the valley, and the town serves as a processing center for *maguey* sap brought in from villages on the nearby slopes.

In its brief history, Benito Juárez has not only become a head town, but has also acquired all the facilities and organizations that are characteristic of small Mexican towns in the early 1970's. The Scalogram of Institutional Complexity (Table 4.3), shows that it possesses all of the items except for a secondary school. Because it has a railroad station, it is ahead of Cerro Grande, which is almost twice as large in population. The acquisition of all these facilities has required, over the years, a concerted effort by the townspeople to mobilize resources in money and labor and to carry their requests to appropriate officials in the state and federal government. The development of the town has also required the investment of outside funds, mostly federal. Local communities in Mexico levy fewer taxes and have less autonomy over their own affairs than do comparable towns in the United States. The development of a community therefore depends on effectiveness in dealing with outside officials as well as on success in organizing the resources—sometimes money and usually labor—that are required as the local contribution for projects such as constructing a water system or building a school.

The growth of the school in Benito Juárez illustrates the roles of both local and outside people. The school was established in 1933, only a year after the founding of the *ejido*, with funds furnished by the Ministry of Public Education in the national government. During the early years, only a minority of the children were enrolled, and those who were generally received only a year or two of education. By 1943 the enrollment had grown to more than 150, and the original building was rebuilt and enlarged by the men of the community (Schensul 1972:7). A decade later, the growth in population stimulated by the new town placed still a greater burden on the facilities. Soon the building could no longer accommodate the rising flood of students, so some classes were held in private homes.

Overcrowding became a major concern of the *Padres de Familia*, the "Parents' Association." This organization is a standard fixture of Mexican schools, but the level of activity varies greatly from community to community. It is not readily comparable to the PTA in the United States, because it is a much more important source of financial support for school

activities and facilities. Money is raised by fund-raising projects
and by contributions from each family.

The Parents' Association in Benito Juárez concentrated first
on acquiring better facilities. Some of the funds raised by this
group have been used as the local contribution required by the
federal government's program of school construction and
expansion. Through these combined efforts the school has been
greatly enlarged during the past ten years, although it is still
crowded because enrollment has continued to grow: it reached
880 by 1969.

Many of the school facilities have been constructed or
purchased with funds raised by the parents. There is an
equipped playground, an outdoor theater, and an elaborate
outdoor loudspeaker system. But the efforts of the Parents'
Association did not stop with bricks and mortar and equipment.
Over the past ten years it has helped to defray the salaries of
eight new teachers, although in Mexico local contributions to
teachers' salaries are unusual. Most salaries are paid by the
federal government, some by the state. The exceptional activity
and success of the Parents' Association in Benito Juárez are
highly accurate indications of the community's commitment to
education.

As in Cerro Grande, the next step up in the scale of
institutional complexity would be the establishment of a
secondary school. The local Committee on Public Works has
mobilized parental support for an effort to obtain such a
school, but so far the municipal president has not been willing
to take such a request to higher authorities (Schensul 1972:12).

It is interesting to compare Benito Juárez with Cerro
Grande, but the differences are not a simple matter of new
versus old, modern versus traditional. Although Benito Juárez is
newer than Cerro Grande and more modern in appearance, it is
much less urban in atmosphere, primarily because it is less
commercial. Cerro Grande has a relatively large market for both
its own population and that of the new town, and it serves as
the secondary trading center in the Valley, behind Los Llanos.
Benito Juárez is a minor trading center, serving many of the
needs of its residents and of nearby villages, although since
1950 it has witnessed the establishment of most of the kinds of
enterprises founded in Cerro Grande during the same period

(Gold 1968:45). The only exceptions are a beverage wholesaler, a coffin maker, and dry cleaner. Nevertheless, the number of stores in the larger town is much greater, and it is this volume that creates the different atmospheres in the two communities.

Until now we have considered only community-level variables; that is, features of the community as an entity in its own right. These features include size of population, the distribution of occupations, institutional complexity, and commercial development. But there is another dimension on which we can compare communities; this dimension is a broad range of individual-level variables, or characteristics of members of the population considered as individuals. In the survey of households the respondents were asked a variety of questions about both their attitudes and opinions and about their behavior. Some of these data will be analyzed more systematically later in this book; here I simply want to add a further contrast to the comparison of the two town centers.

The questions about attitudes were designed, in part, to elicit information about modern versus traditional values with respect to family organization, sex roles, the chances for success in life, planning for the future, and parents' aspirations for their children. The questions about behavior dealt with various aspects of participation in the wider society. This rather broad notion of articulation encompasses political activity, membership in organizations, exposure to the mass media, and contact with urban places, especially Mexico City.

Our analysis of the interviews has shown that, in general, age, education, and occupation are more important determinants of values and behavior than the community in which an individual lives. Furthermore, these factors tend to reinforce each other. Factory workers are the most modern group in the smaller towns and villages, partly because of their occupation, but also because they tend to be younger and better educated than members of other groups. The lesser importance of community as a determinant of values and behavior is illustrated by the fact that factory workers in Benito Juárez, for example, have more in common with their co-workers who live in Cerro Grande than they have with the farmers who are their fellow townsmen in Benito Juárez. Still, if we compare factory workers in Benito Juárez with those in Cerro Grande, and do the same with farmers, we observe that the towns are somewhat different. The poeple of Benito Juárez tend to hold more modern attitudes and values, and are more highly articulated with the wider society. They participate more actively in politics, belong to more organizations, listen to the radio more frequently, read more newspapers, and visit Mexico City more often. But in this case these differences are not large; the other social factors mentioned above are more significant than place of residence.

The contrasting characters of the two town centers in the survey emerge rather clearly from the variety of comparative data. Cerro Grande is somewhat more urban in three ways: (1) it is larger; (2) it has a lower percentage of farmers and a higher percentage of factory workers and other occupations; and (3) although its stores are only slightly more varied, they are much more numerous, and the level of commercial activity is consequently greater. On the other hand, Benito Juárez is the more modern community in two ways: (1) it appears to be more dynamic because it ranks slightly higher in institutional complexity, even though it is smaller and much newer; and (2) its people are more modern in their attitudes and values and more closely articulated with the wider society.

Cristóbal. Like many villages in the region, Cristóbal is built around an ex-hacienda. The imposing estate house with its walled compound stands in the center of the community, abandoned as a dwelling, but in partial use as a storehouse for grain. A wide grass area in front of the house is crossed by rutted roads, and on the other side are a few small shops. The easy pace of life reveals itself in the small group of men that might be seen chatting outside one of the shops; but the village's ties with the outside world are evident when a steady stream of workers return home after the factories of Ciudad Industrial close at 4:30.

The labor force in Cristóbal includes a greater percentage of factory workers than that of any other community in the network, except for the new town (Table 5.1). Some of these men are natives of the village, but most have moved in from outside the region. This influx has produced a high rate of growth over the past twenty years, second only to Cerro Grande.

The hacienda was originally one of the region's middle-sized estates: its decaying buildings are substantial but not nearly as grand and elegant as those of the estate which gave its land, however unwillingly, to form Benito Juárez. The *ejido* of Cristóbal was established in 1939, later than most others in the area. It was formed by peons of this hacienda, of the hacienda in Roca Vista, and of another nearby. They were later joined by some of the people from other parts of the country who came into the region seeking land. The *ejido* lands consist of approximately 1,000 acres of some of the best land in the valley. The land is too valuable to grow much *maguey,* so no *pulque* is produced in the village. In Cristóbal, as in the rest of the valley, the major crops are corn and barley. Two old, unused irrigation canals testify to the long-standing importance of agriculture.

A good gravel road about one-half mile long connects Cristóbal with the paved highway that runs south from the new town. The frequent bus service on the highway includes two buses a day that are routed through the village itself. One of the features of traditional design in the area is that streets are not cobblestone unless they need to be, that is, unless they are on a slope and therefore need protection against washing away during the rains of summer. Since Cristóbal lies on land that is perfectly flat, all of its streets—which might better be labeled broad pathways between rows of houses—are of dirt, with grass where it has not been worn away.

Cristóbal has the distinction of a water system that was originally built in 1943 by the cooperative labor of the residents. When the pump powered by a gasoline engine broke down, the system was tied into the water supply of Ciudad Industrial, thereby forming another of many bonds with the new town. The system was enlarged and the mains extended during 1968-1969. Electricity was installed in 1955, and was largely financed by the construction company that built the new town.

Not all of the facilities in Cristóbal came from the largesse of the government and the new town. The school was constructed in 1945 with local labor and a contribution of 100 pesos (eight dollars) from every head of household and every other adult male. Local people have also built two houses for teachers, as well as offices for the *ejido*. The church, completed in 1957, was also constructed by some of the local citizens.

In the Scale of Institutional Complexity, Cristóbal has the first nine items. The next item in the scale is a full primary school. It may be a long time before the community acquires that item, because of the proximity of Ciudad Industrial, where they go after the third grade, and where they have a better education available than do children in most other villages. Ties with the new town have been a mixed blessing for Cristóbal as they are for Cerro Grande. New facilities and new opportunities are nearby, but they also act as a brake on the further development of the community. Cristóbal is one of the few villages in the network that acquired no new scale items between 1958 and 1966. It should be said that some important items, such as a church and electricity, were added shortly before 1958.

The proximity of Ciudad Industrial has also hampered Cristóbal's commercial development. The only local shops are several very small general stores (called *miscelaneas* in Mexico), a small butcher shop, a small bakery, and a mill for grinding corn into flour for *tortillas*, the staple of the Mexican diet. Of these, the only one added since 1958 is the bakery. (This type of shop is symbolical of the process of modernization: to oversimplify a bit, bread is a "middle class" food while *tortillas* are a "peasant" food. This statement needs to be qualified with a further explanation. Almost everyone in Mexico eats *tortillas* on some occasions, and it is the staple for most of the population. Yet most people also aspire to vary their diet with bread; in recent decades the proportion of the population that consumes some bread has risen steadily.)

Cristóbal's lack of growth contrasts sharply with the great commercial expansion of the town centers in the area. It is especially notable in the light of population growth. Although more people are involved in agriculture than in any other occupation, Cristóbal has become something of a "bedroom suburb" for the new town. In this respect it differs greatly from its "twin" village, Rocavista.

Rocavista. On the other side of the highway from Cristóbal, a short distance up the lower slopes of the mountain in the middle of the valley, the houses of Rocavista also surround an ex-hacienda. They are scattered haphazardly, and the familiar grid pattern of streets (or at least paths) is lacking. Although the estate house is smaller than that in Cristóbal, the hacienda was no less important. Because of the political influence of its owner, it was not expropriated until 1938, late in the period of intensive land reform.

Although the village's location on a rocky hillside does not appear to be favorable for agriculture, it is nevertheless reasonably well endowed with good land. The *ejido* has about 2,200 acres, 75 percent of which are on the valley floor. The remaining land on the mountainside is used for pasture and for the cultivation of a modest amount of *maguey*, whose sap is processed in two one-room fermentation plants in the village.

Rocavista is the most thoroughly agricultural of all the settlements within the shadow of the new town; and, except for San Manuel, it is the most agricultural community in the survey. Four-fifths of the work force is farmers or farm workers. With a total population of 418 in 1970, it is also the smallest community in the survey.

The road to Rocavista symbolizes its relationship to the world beyond. Yard for yard, it is one of the worst roads in the network: parallel ruts made by tires pick their way around the exposed bedrock and through the mud holes. Virtually impassable to passenger cars at any time, it is difficult even for trucks during the rainy season. But the village is only half a mile off the highway, so the residents have an easy walk to the excellent bus service there.

Rocavista has electricity, but it lacks a modern water system. There is a man-made pond, and many houses have cisterns that catch rainwater, the supply of which is ample only during the summer and early fall. A water system is not an item in the Scale of Institutional Complexity because it does not fit consistently with the other items.

The scale is a useful instrument for comparing all the communities in the network, but it is not a sharp enough tool for differentiating those that are similar in many respects. For example, Rocavista and Cristóbal are ranked side by side on the scale, differing only in that the latter has a railroad station. Yet there are some finer differences that do now show up in the scale. The church in Cristóbal was built by the community, while the people of Rocavista use the chapel of the ex-hacienda, although they do keep it in good repair.

Although the school in Rocavista was built in 1949-50, a little later than the one in Cristóbal, the residents made the same kind of personal contributions. Yet in 1958 there was no teacher, and the school was not functioning. By the early 1960's a teacher had been hired, and now the village has three grades, the same number as in Cristóbal. Most of the pupils who attend beyond the third grade go to Ciudad Industrial and the rest go to Cerro Grande.

The condition of commerce in Rocavista is exactly the same as that in Cristóbal: there are a few *miscelaneas*, a corn mill, a butcher shop, and a bakery. The latter two have been added since 1958.

To summarize this comparison of the two villages, perhaps the most important difference lies in the roles that they play in the immediate region. Cristóbal, by serving as home for an increasing number of factory workers, has developed a unique relationship with the new town. Rocavista, on the other hand, continues as an agricultural village dedicated to corn, barley, and to some extent, *pulque*.

Santa Cecilia. Up a gentle slope behind Benito Juárez, the new water tower of Santa Cecilia stands as a symbol of progress. Since the tank is red, the tower has earned the nickname of *El Gallo*, "the rooster." Santa Cecilia is one of the few villages in the valley that is not built around an ex-hacienda as a nucleus. There is an abandoned hacienda nearby, but it dates from the sixteenth century and the days when the Valley of Los Llanos was devoted to the raising of cattle to help feed the growing Spanish and Creole population of Mexico City. A memorial to an earlier style of architecture, the thick walls and massive buttresses of the estate house are all that remain.

Farther up the slope is one of the most interesting remains of the heyday of *pulque*. The ex-hacienda of Malpais, built by a person with a knack for integrating architecture with the landscape, commands a low pass into a natural amphitheater in the hills. The original trail passes through an elegant gateway down the slope and proceeds about a quarter of a mile to the hacienda. The estate house, small by local standards, is of pleasing scale and design, with a second-story balcony across the front and around three sides of the patio. Some rooms are used for grain and storage, the rest of the house is abandoned to the pigs and chickens, and small trees grow from the roof. The remains of wide sidewalks and steps made from black lava lead to outbuildings that seem to merge with the rocks on the hillsides.

Peons from Malpais joined with some from two other haciendas to found Santa Cecilia in the mid-1930's. The original allocation of land, 2,350 acres, was divided among 108 members and their families after 500 acres were set aside as communal land to benefit the whole village. These 500 acres were on the mountainside and suitable only for pasture and *maguey*, yet they were sufficiently productive that the proceeds allowed the community to build a school in 1937, one of the first *ejido* schools in the region. The land base of the community was expanded by 660 additional acres in 1939.

Santa Cecilia has not grown much since it was formed by those original 108 families. Many of the offspring of those families have left in search of better opportunities for education, employment, or marriage. Today there are fewer families, slightly under 100, but they tend to be larger, so that the population was 569 in 1970.

The village is connected to the highway by a better-than-average dirt road, and the people walk its 2½ mile length to the buses for Los Llanos, Ciudad Industrial, and points beyond. Table 4.3 shows that Santa Cecilia, lacking electricity, ranks a step below Rocavista in institutional complexity. That deficiency was soon overcome by the completion of an electrical system in 1968. In the domain of commerce, the village has the four basic enterprises found in the other villages.

There are three patterns of relationship between haciendas and the *ejidos* that were formed during the land reform. Santa Cecilia represents one, in which the peons moved away to build a new village on their new lands. In some of these cases, the haciendas continue to operate, although on a scale much reduced from their former grandeur. Cristóbal and Rocavista represent another pattern, in which the haciendas were expropriated in their entirety and therefore abandoned completely. The third pattern might be called peaceful coexistence. In these cases, the peons received most of the land and stayed in their houses in the shadow of the hacienda walls, while the estate continued to operate with whatever holdings remained in its possession. The rarity of this sort of arrangement should come as no surprise, since it seems to presuppose a high degree of good feeling between former master and former peon. The only example in the Valley of Los Llanos is Adonde.

Adonde. At the southern edge of the valley, beside the highway between Benito Juárez and Los Llanos, the high-walled compound of the old estate looms above the adobe houses of the former peons and their descendants. The hacienda, which was reduced during the land reform to the legal maximum of 200 hectares (494 acres), no longer produces *pulque*. Its good bottom land is used, as throughout the valley, for corn, barley, and beans. In some ways the owner continues to act as patron of the community. He keeps the chapel in good repair, and it serves as the local church. The village water supply is taken from the hacienda's well, and the only charge is the cost of the electricity for running the pump. The owner gives an annual feast for the village, the setting for which is the large banquet hall, which is now in a state of disrepair but which preserves something of its former elegance.

After most of the hacienda was expropriated in 1937, two separate *ejidos* were formed, one by local people and the other by peons from a hacienda about ten miles to the northeast. The national census enumerates each *ejido* separately. Each has a name, and each has its own commissioner and judge. But the two administrations work closely together, and all of the local services and facilities are shared. So, in charts and tables, I am treating the community as a single entity.

Although Adonde is primarily agricultural, among the villages in the survey it is second only to Cristóbal in numbers of factory workers. They commute daily by bus to the new town. The *ejidos* were founded by a total of 170 families, who would have formed a total population of about 800. That figure has now more than doubled with a 1970 population of 1,744. The total land holdings are 3,000 acres, of which 2,000 are on the valley bottom. All of the cash crops of the region are grown on the good land, and the rest produces a considerable amount of *maguey* sap which is processed in three small fermentation plants.

In institutional complexity, Adonde ranks above the other villages because it has a full primary school. The factories in the new town have assisted the community by helping to obtain additional teachers. Commercial growth has lagged behind the development of facilities and institutions, no doubt because of the proximity of Los Llanos, the trade center of the network. Adonde has the same kinds of shops as the smaller villages in our study; at the time of the Youngs' research in 1958, the only type of store present was the *miscelanea*.

All of the communities discussed so far have some factory workers, although less than ten percent of the work force in Rocavista and Santa Cecilia is in that occupation. We also wanted to include in the survey a community with no industrial employees. For this purpose we selected San Manuel, a village in the northeastern part of the *municipio* of Cerro Grande.

San Manuel. San Manuel is the most isolated and most agricultural community represented in the survey of households. Except for a handful of shopkeepers, all of the labor force consists of farmers or farm workers. During parts of the rainy season, even rugged second-class buses have difficulty with the dirt road that runs from Cerro Grande to San Manuel and on to the northeast. Whenever the road is not totally impassable, there is one bus per day in each direction from San Manuel.

The village sits on the north side of a shallow lake that is a remnant of Pleistocene times, when the world was wetter and the central Mexican plateau was not a semi-desert. In those days the entire Valley of Los Llanos was a lake, and silt was deposited to form the good farmland that is on the valley floor today. Although the weed-choked lake yields a few fish, it is better noted for a plentiful supply of ducks, and there is a hunting club with a clubhouse.

There are three clusters of houses in San Manuel, the most important of which surrounds the school, church, clubhouse, and largest general store. The clubhouse also serves as headquarters for the *ejido* and as a meeting hall. There is another neighborhood to the east, and the third is northwest, somewhat up the hillside and looking out across the lake.

The *ejido* was established in 1935 and now holds about 1,400 acres. Most of this is bottom land that produces corn and barley. Little *maguey* sap is collected and there is no processing of *pulque* in the village. From time to time local men have worked in the factories as temporary laborers under a provision of the national labor law which states that employers may hire workers for a period not exceeding thirty days, without having to give them an fringe benefits or rights of tenure. None of the men from San Manuel has succeeded in obtaining a regular, continuing post.

With no change in the economic base of the community, a low rate of population growth would be expected; but a rate of 9 percent in two decades (see Table 5.1) is strikingly low, especially in light of the fact that the rest of the nation doubled in size during the same period. So little growth is a result, not of few births, but of much migration. Lacking opportunities in their natal villages, young people leave to seek work in Mexico City and other urban centers. This pattern occurs elsewhere in the region, but not so extensively, because elsewhere the new town has boosted local economies.

Of the communities in the survey, San Manuel ranks lowest in institutional complexity. Its highest scale item is a school, which has three grades. The building of the church took a long time—1937 to 1963—but it was accomplished entirely with local funds and local labor. The kinds of stores available are the same as in the other villages, but the variety of goods stocked is considerably less. For example, in one or another general store in Cristóbal, the consumer can buy flavored ice bars, shoes, cloth, blankets, whitewash, building cement, or motor oil. None of these is available in San Manuel.

San Manuel is relatively isolated and has not benefitted economically from the emergence of the new town. On the other hand, it has a reasonable amount of good land, and it has been exporting its surplus population to cities outside the region. The survey of households shows that the standard of living is no worse than that of most farming groups in the area, and a bit better than some.

These seven towns and villages represent the range of variation in the region. They vary in size, facilities, the distribution of occupations, and the importance of the traditional product, *pulque*. Yet behind this diversity is a common pattern of social structure, the principles of which will be described in the next chapter.

CHAPTER SIX

Village Social Structure

In the communities of the Valley of Los Llanos, social relationships are ordered, as they are throughout Mexico, by three fundamental institutions: the family, *compadrazgo* (the total complex of godparenthood), and the system of social stratification.

From the villager's point of view, the family is the most important social unit. From the anthropologist's point of view, the most important structural feature depends on the purpose of his study. At the risk of oversimplifying, I would say that the family is clearly the most significant *group* in village society, but that the stratification system is more important for locating the village and its elements within the structure of the nation.

It is important to keep in mind the difference between the family and the household. The various types of families are groups of people related in one way or another by ties of marriage and descent. The household is the group of people who live together and who act in some way as an economic unit; that is, as a unit of consumption and sometimes as a unit of production. The household, in Mexico as in many other societies, usually consists of a family and no one else; but sometimes it includes godchildren, friends, or distant relatives who are not members of the immediate family.

Actually it is not sufficient to define the household as the people who live together, since there are different degrees of living together. In the household survey that was an important part of our research, we let each respondent define the household herself (questions about these matters were asked of women only) simply by listing its members. This procedure showed that the household is not seen simply in terms of the buildings that it occupies, but is defined as the group that uses the same kitchen and therefore acts as an economic unit, at least in this limited sense. Seen this way, about three-fourths of all households in the area consist of a nuclear family. Most of the rest are nuclear families with one or more members added: an elderly parent, a niece or nephew, some other relative, or a godchild. It is relatively uncommon to see a household with a full-scale extended family consisting of three generations: grandparents, parents, and children. Only seven percent of the households in the sample are of this sort.

Now I want to make it clear that the structural predominance of the nuclear over the extended family is not as great as these figures suggest. The figures refer to the composition of households as it was described by the female respondents, who were in almost all cases the wives of the men defined as heads of the households. Few extended families live together in the sense that they use the same kitchen. But more live together in the sense that they are arranged around the same compound. An example will make the difference clear.

On the outskirts of Cerro Grande, in a neighborhood occupied by members of an *ejido*, is the home of Alfonso Velasco, a man in his early 60's and a charter member of the *ejido*. His compound occupies about one-fourth of a square block, to use a North American measurement. He and his wife live in the original (and largest) house, whose main room also serves as the living and dining room for family fiestas and other social occasions. The Velascos' three children are all married and all live in the compound with their own children. Each has built his or her own house with kitchen and bedrooms only, since the parents' house serves as the social area. The members of this large extended family see themselves as comprising four households, each with its own head, united in the compound headed by Alfonso Velasco. Each household is composed of a nuclear family whose members sleep under the same roof and ordinarily use their own kitchens. The parents' kitchen is used communally only on special occasions.

The important point in this example is that there are two

levels of organization. The nuclear family is a unit unto itself for some purposes, while in other ways several such families are united in a higher-order unit. The Valasco extended family is interesting for other reasons: it has made a highly successful adaptation to changing circumstances. The father and his two sons all work for the industries in the new town, while the son-in-law runs the agricultural operations of the entire group.

Compadrazgo

Another fundamental institution in the social organization is the system of *compadrazgo*, which is one of the world's best-known examples of what anthropologists call "ritual kinship." *Compadrazgo* could be translated literally as "co-parenthood": it refers to the complex of relationships established by the custom of selecting godparents as sponsors for baptisms and other ceremonial events. The system was important in Medieval Europe, where it has persisted most strongly in the less industrialized areas such as Spain and the Balkans (Mintz and Wolf 1950:352). The Spanish carried it to the New World where it has spread widely and developed diverse forms.

The selection of godparents establishes two sets of relationships, those between the child and his sponsors and those between the parents and the sponsors. In North American culture the former is rather widespread, but there is little emphasis on and no common label for the relationship of "co-parents." This latter tie is the more important in Mexico and throughout Latin America. The parents and the sponsors call each other *compadre* ("co-father") and *comadre* ("co-mother") and recognize obligations of solidarity and mutual assistance. The godparents also assume some responsibilities for the religious and moral education of their godchild, but the most salient relationship and the most significant interaction is among the four co-parents.

Within the broader social structure, the *compadrazgo* system can be used either to strengthen already existing ties of kinship or friendship, or to create new relationships, frequently with persons of higher status. It can also vary with respect to its orientation toward the community: ties may be concentrated within the village, or they may extend beyond the village to other groups.

In the Los Llanos region, *compadrazgo* largely serves to cement existing bonds, and *compadres* are overwhelmingly friends rather than relatives. The household survey contains information on 784 relationships. Only 11 percent of the *compadres* are also relatives, while 83 percent are identified as friends. As a way of acquiring some social capital, a couple will sometimes ask a higher status couple to be godparents; but this pattern is not important numerically, although it may be highly significant in individual cases. The total number of *compadre* ties is very large; only 40 percent cross community boundaries, but this volume is large enough to be a major means of inter-village contact.

Social Stratification

The dominant tradition of anthropological work in Mexico has overemphasized the homogeneity of the community. Anthropologists, after all, tend to study some of the smallest and most homogeneous communities, the Indian villages. In contrast to larger, more urban places, these villages certainly seem to lack internal diversity. Redfield's well-known book on Yucatán (1941) applied the notion of the folk-urban continuum to Mexico. Partly because he compared two villages with a town and a city, Redfield overstated the homogeneity of the villages. Even small places manifest systematic social inequalities, although anthropologists frequently underplay them in their attempts to present an "inside view" of a culture—and those inequalities are not part of the villagers' own image of their community.

In Chapter 2, I explained briefly the nature of social stratification in pre-Revolutionary Mexico. In less than half a century, the nation changed from a traditional society with a small elite at the top and a large mass of peasants at the base to a modernizing society with new sources of wealth, power, and prestige. In relatively stable, agrarian societies, the definition of social classes seems rather clear-cut: there is no particular problem in distinguishing the landed gentry from the peasants.

In industrial societies, however, and especially in rapidly industrializing ones, it is not so easy to define classes. The delineation of status is just as important, but it tends to assume the form of a continuum from top to bottom, where the lines between levels or "classes" are drawn somewhat arbitrarily. A "social class" is a convenient label for a segment of the continuum.

Using a simple scheme of upper, middle, and popular classes in Table 6.1, Gonzáles Cosío (1961) has documented the changes in Mexican stratification during this century. He defines the upper class as the large landowners and the business, professional, and governmental elite. The middle class includes skilled workers and artisans as well as the usual merchants, white-collar workers, and technicians. The popular class consists of the majority of the population: small farmers and unskilled manual workers. Although the figures in Table 6.1 are not as precise as the decimal places suggest, they nevertheless convey the major changes that have taken place in Mexico. The upper class has shrunk slightly and has shifted overwhelmingly from a

Table 6.1. The Changing Class Profile of Mexico

	1900	1960
Upper Class		
Urban	0.2%	0.4%
Rural	0.4	0.1
Subtotal	0.6	0.5
Middle Class		
Urban	1.7	7.2
Rural	6.6	9.9
Subtotal	8.3	17.1
Popular Class		
Urban	16.3	32.3
Rural	74.8	50.1
Subtotal	91.1	82.4
TOTAL	100.0%	100.0%

(González Cosío 1961:55)

rural, landowning base to urban areas. The peasants have not disappeared, but their structural position in the system has changed in that their labor is no longer the principal source of wealth. Roughly speaking, the peasants are the rural segment of the popular class, which has declined from three-fourths to one-half of the population. The middle class has grown, and appears in the table to be primarily rural only because artisans and petty merchants are included.

This emergence of a middle stratum is perhaps the most important change. This group is the spearhead for an ideology of modernization, which emphasizes the possibilities of progress through technology for society as a whole, and of greater equality for the individual through education and social mobility. The desired mobility is facilitated by the continuing development of a modern occupational system, in which work increasingly takes place in impersonal organizations rather than in the family firm that is so characteristic of farmers and artisans. Without any training in the social sciences, rural people have come to recognize the great structural importance of the occupational system. Their awareness is reflected in their growing disillusionment with traditional vocations such as farming and shopkeeping, and in their increasingly (and unrealistically) high aspirations for their children. These changes will be documented in Chapters 7 and 8.

The system of social stratification is a national system that is reflected in various ways at the village level, and some of the changes that have taken place in the nation have also occurred in the region of Los Llanos. These changes have been produced, both nationally and locally, by the Revolution and by industrialization. In some ways the Revolution destroyed the local class system by eliminating the domination and control exercised by the *pulque* haciendas. But in other ways the uneven distribution of wealth, power, and prestige persisted in a modified but recognizable form.

The owners of the great estates, who had been a tiny elite poised at the pinnacle of local society, saw most of their economic base removed by the land reform. Some were able to preserve a degree of local prominence by continuing to operate their greatly reduced haciendas. Others maintained an elite position in Mexico City by expanding their roles in the distribution of *pulque* or by other enterprises. But the local importance of the traditional elite was severely undercut by the Revolution.

As I explained in Chapter Two, the land reform gave a new kind of independence to the *pulque* tappers and the small farmers of the area; but it did not solve their economic problems, and it left their lowly position in the class system essentially unchanged. No matter how the limited resources of the region were divided up, they were insufficient to support a more comfortable life. To be sure, the redistribution of land was a redistribution of wealth, but the total income-producing potential of the land was reduced by several factors: the loss of the efficiencies of large-scale operation in the hacienda system; the continuing decline of the *pulque* industry; and the constraint that the uncertain climate placed on the production of the barley, the major alternate crop. The prestige of the lowest-status groups also remained unchanged. The intellectuals of the Revolution affirmed the dignity of the Indian and the peasant; and the great muralists—Orozco, Rivera, and Siquieros—captured that dignity on the walls of public buildings and hotels in the capital city. Yet, to the man on the street (or on the country trail), the work of the farmer, and especially that of the *pulque* tapper, was characterized more by drudgery than by dignity. Only in the domain of power did the people on the land improve their position. The Revolution gave them control of their own communities (the *ejidos*), and peasants came to exercise more national influence in the halls of government.

Before the land reform, the middle level of local society— the managers of haciendas and the small businessmen—had been almost as small as the elite. They were affected perhaps least of all by the changes of the 1930's. Some managers continued to administer estates that survived on a reduced scale; others established their own one-room breweries in old villages or in new *ejidos*. Still others shifted their arena of work to *pulque* distribution systems, which remained in private hands. With the disappearance of the hacienda stores that had been the pillar of the debt-bondage system, opportunities for local merchants increased somewhat, but they were still severely limited by the low income levels in the region.

The decline of the *pulque* industry and the unreliability of the climate combined to create an agriculture that was increasingly marginal and a local economy that was increasingly depressed. The villages of the region were rather grim, seedy places: the streets were dusty or muddy, depending on the season; the houses were small and ill-kept; and the stores were most conspicuous by their absence. In this scene of growing despair, a new town was built. It created a whole new set of possibilities for survival.

CHAPTER SEVEN

The Development of Ciudad Industrial

One might wonder why three large factories and a new town were built in the barley fields of a semi-arid plain in central Mexico. There were two primary considerations involved in the decision to proceed with the project. One was the realization that the region was suffering severe economic problems. The governor of the state, an influential man in national politics, forcefully brought these problems to the attention of officials in Mexico City. The other consideration was the growing concern about the accelerating rate of concentration of industry and people in Mexico City itself. An official booklet about Ciudad Industrial explains that it was planned as a:

> ... solution to the necessity for the economic transformation of the country, that is now demanding the construction of planned industrial nuclei.
>
> This fulfillment of this goal constitutes an unequivocal response to the evidence that identified the state of Hidalgo as a zone of economic deficiency with a marked tendency to crises, because of its dependence on two types of production: mining and *pulque*.
>
> Coinciding with this situation, there was an outflow of capital to Mexico City and a displacement of population toward new centers of employment located in surrounding states [translation by the author].

I have already described in some detail the economic problems of the research region. For anyone who has visited Mexico City in recent years, the degree of concentration there needs no description. Month by month the population grows, the traffic increases, and the smog becomes more acrid. The spectacular increase of population in the Federal District, which more or less corresponds to the metropolitan area of Mexico City, is shown by these figures (Benítez Zenteno and Cabrera Acevedo 1966).

1900	400,000
1930	1,000,000
1970	7,100,000
1980 (projected)	11,300,000

The economic and cultural predominance of Mexico City, and the increasing degree of concentration there, are even more spectacular:

	1940	1955	1960
Federal District's share of national population	8.0%	—	13.3%
Federal District's share of industrial output	37.8%	48.1%	—

(Adapted from Yates 1961)

By comparison, Hidalgo and the seven other least industrialized states accounted for only 5.6 percent of the output in 1940, and this figure declined to a pathetic 3.3 percent by 1955, although they had 24.7 percent of the nation's population in that year. There were even more striking differences in industrial output per worker. In 1955, the figure for the Federal District was seventeen times higher than for Hidalgo, the state in which the new town is located.

These kinds of discrepancies could be documented statistically to the point of boredom. Twenty years ago, as economists and planners in the federal government were becoming concerned about such facts, two new firms were seeking locations for their factories. One of these was to produce railroad cars, the other to assemble automobiles, buses, and trucks. Both were formed by "state participation," as they say in Mexico; that is, they were publicly owned. The Valley of Los Llanos already had some of the infrastructure required by heavy industry: power, lines, a pipeline for natural gas, and the intersection of two railroads.

The situation was studied by the Bank of Mexico (Mexico's central bank) and *Nacional Financiera,* a publicly owned development bank that has been very successful in stimulating and financing industrialization (Aubey 1966; Blair 1964). Taking into account the economic needs of the State of Hidalgo, the growing problems of centralization in Mexico City, the existence of technological facilities, and the urgings of the Governor of Hidalgo, these institutions joined in recommending that both firms locate in the Valley of Los Llanos, near the electric, gas, and rail lines.

The automotive firm quickly accepted the recommendation, and began to build both the factory and housing for its personnel. It also adopted the policy of buying all possible materials and provisions in the state rather than in Mexico City. The railroad firm, after analyzing the facilities of the region, concluded that there was a fundamental problem in the absence of amenities that would lure highly skilled labor away from more urban areas. It decided to make its choice of location conditional on the solution of this problem.

The next development in the unfolding drama was an idea of the Subdirector of the Bank of Mexico: to build a new town in order to create an agreeable, modern environment for the personnel of the factories. The idea was received with enthusiasm. On the seventeenth of June, 1952, a construction firm was created by presidential decree to develop the new community. The importance of the effort is suggested by the fact that the Director of *Nacional Financiera* became the Director General of the new enterprise.

The project was begun with enthusiasm and high hopes. As the official booklet said:

> . . . an industrial city to resolve the problem of integrating the industrial and residential sectors, through suitable planning, was in effect an experiment, but one that could constitute a definitive phase in the socio-economic evolution of Mexico [translation by the author].

Design and Construction of the New Town

Ciudad Industrial looks neat, orderly, and, frankly, monotonous. The factories are not housed in the handsome structures that some industries have built in Mexico. They look like factories, but nevertheless they contain most of the interesting architecture in the community (see Plate 9). Those symbols of industrial advance, high tension lines, cut directly through the middle of the residential area. The houses are arranged in careful rows along parallel streets. The newest ones are detached structures of brick, but most of the town consists of hundreds of rows of concrete houses which have a common wall with the houses on either side (see Plate 12). Each row faces another row across a strip of grass and trees. Literally thousands of trees were planted where virtually none had grown before.

The monotony of the rows is emphasized by the flat concrete roofs, each with a concrete water tank on top, and all but a few with television antennae. On the other hand, it is relieved somewhat by the many pastel colors of the exterior walls. All houses have hot and cold running water and bathrooms with showers and flush toilets. Such facilities are still luxuries for most Mexicans, especially for factory workers.

Map 2 shows the general plan of the town. The design work was completed rapidly, within five months after the formation of the construction company. The community was built in stages: 694 houses by 1955, and 615 more by 1958. The costs (in dollars) were:

Land	$ 192,000
Streets and highways	1,112,000
Utilities and public services	1,136,000
Public buildings and markets	440,000
Housing	2,840,000
Total	$5,720,000

Although all the houses appear to be similar, there is considerable variation in the size and cost of individual units. The smallest, built especially for unskilled workers, have only 340 square feet of living area and were built to rent for only $9.00 a month, although that figure has gone up to $11.00. The largest houses for factory workers are slightly more than twice as large, and they rent for about twice as much. To interpret these figures, it is necessary to know that unskilled workers now make $40–$60 a month, and skilled workers make $100–$200.

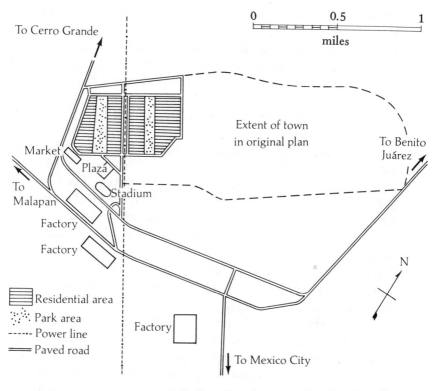

To Cerro Grande

0   0.5   1

miles

Extent of town
in original plan

Market

Plaza

To Benito
Juárez

To
Malapan

Stadium

Factory

Factory

N

▦ Residential area
⋰⋰ Park area
----- Power line
═══ Paved road

Factory

To Mexico City

Map 2.   Sketch-map of Ciudad Industrial.

A few units with many more amenities were built for executives and engineers. They have up to 2,000 square feet of room and now rent for approximately $100 a month.

The complement of housing includes several four-story apartment buildings and several buildings locally called *colectivos* (literally, "collectives"), which might best be labeled dormitories in English. Designed for single workers, they consist of rooms with baths, but not with kitchens. Since there are few restaurants, many dormitory residents cook on hotplates in their rooms.

Some of the public facilities of Ciudad Industrial appear in Map 2. The main square is a typical Mexican plaza in some ways: it has trees, grass, a fountain, and a statue of Father Miguel Hidalgo who issued the call for Mexican independence 160 years ago (see Plate 14). It is surrounded by the municipal building, communications offices (mail, telegraph, and telephone), and the church. But it is very atypical in that it is off to the side, by itself, between the residential and industrial zones, three blocks from the nearest houses. Consequently, it is not the hub of social interaction that most Mexican plazas are, and usually the only people around are those who have come on business to one of the public buildings.

Another strikingly atypical feature of the new town is the church itself (see Plate 16). Its utter simplicity, standing in sharp contrast to the elegant colonial structures of nearby towns, dramatically symbolizes both a change in Mexican culture and a characteristic of Ciudad Industrial. The former is the decline in the institutional importance of the Catholic Church that has accompanied the secularism of the Revolution; and the latter is the weak sense of community in the new town. Many of its residents participate in religious activities in their home towns, rather than devote their time and money to building a church that would be appropriate to the size and importance of Ciudad Industrial.

Other public facilities are also located between the residential and industrial zones. The market is the center of daily activity. A building that occupies about one-quarter of a square block houses permanent shops and small lunch counters. Outside there is a larger concrete apron with benches for the large market every Saturday. The people of the community, unlike the typical Mexican town-dweller, are unable to keep domestic animals on the house sites or to have gardens. Their numbers include a proportion of children that is higher than the average in the country, and the average is high indeed, since Mexico has one of the fastest rates of population growth in the world. Consequently, Ciudad Industrial has a heavy demand for both food and clothing, a demand which is satisfied principally by the weekly market. On a typical Saturday there are 350 vendors selling an impressive variety of corn, beans, fresh fruits and vegetables, herbs and spices, clothes, shoes, and utensils.

The bus depot is also located at the permanent market building. A steady stream of first- and second-class buses travels to the state capital, to Mexico City, and to local communities.

Between the plaza and the factories are a stadium with a graceful concrete roof and seats for several thousand, squash and *frontón* courts, and soccer fields. The facilities are used

Plates 9 and 10.   A factory and its product

Plates 11 and 12.   Street scenes: a village and the new town
(Plate 11 by Timothy Roufs)

Plates 13 and 14.   Plazas: a village and the new town
(Plate 13 by Timothy Roufs)

Plates 15 and 16.   Churches: a village and
the new town

intensively on weekends by many active sports clubs, and on important national holidays, thousands of school children fill the stadium field to present patriotic pageants, precision calisthenics, and drills.

Demographic Impact on the Region

Ciudad Industrial offers a curious paradox: it was built in part to enhance the economy of a depressed region with a shortage of jobs, and yet most of the workers came from outside the immediate area. The resolution of the paradox is simple: the new factories needed primarily skilled workers and technicians, and there were virtually none in the area. Considering the level of training in the local labor force, it is surprising that so many found jobs in the new town.

Initially, the local workers were hired as unskilled laborers in the construction of the factories and houses. Later, some of them obtained positions in the factories as apprentices, janitors, or other unskilled workers. But the nature of production in the industries demanded large numbers of highly skilled men such as drill press operators, machinists, and welders. Consequently, there was an intensive recruiting campaign to attract men from the national labor market, especially from Mexico City. These men were offered television sets or phonographs as bonuses, and of course there was the additional inducement of low rents in the publicly-owned housing. The result of the campaign was a major influx of people into an economically declining region known in the past as an exporter of surplus population.

Since some knowledge of the origins and compositions of the population is fundamental to an understanding of the nature of all the communities in the area, I shall present data in some detail. The first families moved into the new town in 1955. The population grew steadily for ten years, as these figures show:

1960 (national census)	6,097
1966 (town census)	11,057
1969 (town census)	11,164
1970 (national census)	12,327

After the growth leveled off in the mid-1960's, it did not even keep pace with the natural rate of increase, which, in 1960 in the State of Hidalgo, was 32.5 per thousand (a birth rate of 46.1 minus a death rate of 13.6). If Ciudad Industrial had grown at that rate from 1966 on, assuming no further migration, it would have had a population of 12,566 by 1970. Instead there was only a small amount of immigration that was more than cancelled out by the emigration of young people coming of age in an industrial town that was no longer expanding and could not offer them employment. In addition, the average of the population of the town kept dropping, as the workers' families grew. The percentage of those under 21 grew from 59 percent in 1966 to 62 percent in 1969, compared to a figure of 57 percent for the state as a whole. The absence of older people became even more striking. In 1960—the latest census figures available for this kind of tabulation—10 percent of the state population was over 50, compared to 3 percent of the new town in 1969.

Patterns of migration into and within the region are especially revealing, and Table 7.1 summarizes a large amount of information. The data were obtained from the personnel files of the two largest factories in the summer of 1966; at that time the total number of employees was about 3,450. Unfortunately, complete information was available on only 2,307 individuals. They are not a random sample, but they represent the full range of jobs. The geographic reality is the Valley of Los Llanos, which defines a small natural region. The social reality is the network of communities in the valley. The table lists, in order of size, the ten most important towns and villages in the network, and then lumps the others together. Abbreviations of names appear across the top of the table in the same order. By reading down each column, one can note the birthplaces of the employees who now live in each of these ten places. For example, of the 210 employees living in Cerro Grande, 85 were born there, 17 elsewhere in the network, and 108 outside the network. Reading across each row gives the present residences of those born in each place.

Since the enterprising reader can discern a number of patterns in the data, I shall remark upon only a few. A minority of· employees (877 or about one-third) were born within the network. Perhaps the most striking figure in the table is the

Table 7.1. Birthplaces and Residences of Factory Employees

Birthplace	Residence										Others in Network	Total Born in Each Town and State
	CI	LL	CG	BJ	M	A	C	SM	SC	R		
Ciudad Industrial	0	0	0	0	0	0	0	0	0	0	0	0
Los Llanos	35	176	4	5	0	1	3	0	0	0	1	225
Cerro Grande	22	3	85	3	3	0	2	0	0	0	11	129
Benito Juárez	7	1	0	39	0	0	0	0	0	0	0	47
Malapan	19	4	4	1	249	0	4	0	0	0	0	281
Adonde	0	1	1	1	0	7	0	0	0	0	0	10
Cristóbal	1	1	1	0	2	0	18	0	0	0	1	24
San Manuel	1	1	0	0	0	0	0	0	0	0	0	2
Santa Cecilia	0	0	0	0	0	0	1	0	1	0	0	2
Rocavista	1	0	0	1	0	0	1	0	0	1	0	4
Other Network Villages	10	15	7	1	1	0	0	0	0	0	119	153
Subtotal: residence of those born in network	96	202	102	51	255	8	29	0	1	1	132	877
Others in Hidalgo	426	38	61	7	16	1	12	1	0	0	7	569
Tlaxcala	95	18	7	5	1	0	2	0	0	0	2	130
Puebla	83	17	6	3	2	0	0	0	0	0	3	114
State of Mexico	65	6	10	6	5	0	3	0	0	0	11	106
Federal District	133	11	9	2	8	1	0	0	0	0	1	165
Other States	301	15	15	5	1	0	5	0	0	0	4	346
Subtotal: residence of those born outside of network	1,103	105	108	28	33	2	22	1	0	0	28	1,430
Total Residing in Each Town	1,199	307	210	79	288	10	51	1	1	1	160	2,307

small proportion of these who live in Ciudad Industrial: there are 96, which is only 11 percent of the locals. Furthermore, the overwhelming majority of the natives of each village still live there, as the figures along the diagonal in the top half of the table show. For example, of the 281 employees born in Malapan, 249 still live there; and only 19 have moved to the new town two miles away. Altogether, 80 percent of the locals still live in their home towns and villages.

By contrast, Ciudad Industrial is the home of 77 percent of those who have moved into the region. Most of them came from elsewhere in the State of Hidalgo and from contiguous states, but each state in the nation has furnished at least one person in this group of employees. The only area not represented is the Territory of Baja California South.

Although most "outsiders" have settled in the new town, significant numbers have moved into other towns. Extrapolating from the sample, which represents less than half the employees, we can estimate that over 200 have moved into Los Llanos and the same number into Cerro Grande. As we shall see later, this influx of workers in modern occupations has had a significant effect on the towns and villages of the region.

The Problems

Perhaps the typical new town has more problems—or at least more noticeable problems—than the typical human community. Certainly Brasilia—to take an example that is clearly *not* typical—has been plagued with difficulties throughout its brief life; and no verdicts can yet be handed down about the growing list of new cities in the United States (*Saturday Review* 1971). The great expectations of the Mexican economists and planners who built Ciudad Industrial have been greatly frustrated. An ultimate population of 60,000 was projected, and the original plan called for an appropriate amount of housing. Yet the town has grown very little since 1966, and no further expansion in facilities is planned. A study commissioned by the city administration in 1964 concluded that the principal problems were as follows:

1. The initial cost of the project was high because social benefits were taken into account more than purely economic consideration.
2. There were feelings of uprootedness, boredom, and dissatisfaction among the population.
3. Industrial development and population growth were slow in relation to the original investment.

Part of the trouble lies in faults of design. The designers were careful to provide grass and trees, but it almost seems if they deliberately eliminated all of the charm of traditional Mexican town plans and domestic architecture. The plaza is not in the center of things, but off to the side. There are no small-scale neighborhood plazas or intersections to serve as informal marketplaces. Houses are not built around patios—a humane custom that admits nature into the home but preserves privacy. Instead they have open yards that allow no possibility of privacy.

Some of the policies by which the town is governed also dilute the flavor of Mexican daily life. No *cantinas* ("saloons") are permitted, perhaps partly because the project has been conceived as something of a showplace for foreign visitors and partly because a fondness for alcoholic beverages is thought to have a negative effect on the productivity of industrial workers. It is possible to have towns without saloons in the United States; in fact, they exist and one expects them to be gloomy. But it is hard to imagine a Mexican town without a place where a man can meet his friends, lubricate his friendships, and validate his *machismo* ("manliness"). Ciudad Industrial is Dublin minus pubs or Paris without sidewalk cafes.

Commerce in other goods is also strictly controlled. Business licenses are required and the supply is limited, so there is no bewildering but intriguing proliferation of tiny shops in the front rooms of houses. Street peddlers of *tamales* or ice cream are also scarce. In Ciudad Industrial, as in all Mexican communities, the market is the center of commercial activity; but such activity is concentrated there to an unusual degree.

Since no housing is privately owned, none of the residents has any control over the design of his dwelling. He cannot expand it to suit the needs of a growing family or to accommodate elderly parents or other relatives. It is physically impossible to maintain an extended family in a single house in Ciudad Industrial.

The town is described as "cold" both by many of its residents and by people who live in surrounding communities. They refer both to the chill winds that come down the valley in the winter, and to the total effect of the town's design, the policies of control, the nature of the housing, and the quality of personal relationships. The implications of this image are several. As we have seen, most of the local villagers who have taken jobs in the factories have chosen to maintain residence in their own villages, and significant numbers of outsiders have located there rather than in the town. The executives and engineers were recruited principally from Mexico City, and many of them spend their weekends there, where they have kept their homes and families. Consequently their salaries contribute little to the new town or its region. As a matter of fact, many of the other residents of Ciudad Industrial spend a considerable amount of money in Mexico City. For major purchases of furniture, appliances, and vehicles, they can find a much larger selection at lower prices. In addition, it is close enough to be the center of weekend entertainment, with its huge variety of restaurants, theatres, and night clubs, and its cosmopolitan atmosphere. For anyone who wants a "big night on the town," the only town to consider is the nation's capital.

Perhaps the most direct constraint on the growth of Ciudad Industrial has been the nature of the employment situation as determined by the needs of the factories. The national and international markets for their products and the position of their competitors have fluctuated, and these fluctuations have set limits on their expansion and on their needs for labor. These limits in turn have affected the growth of the new town, whose size depends directly on the number of jobs available.

It is easy to describe the problems in Ciudad Industrial. The manufacturing base did not expand as rapidly as anticipated. The town is too far from Mexico City to be a suburb and too close to be an independent community. Its peculiarities of both physical and social design make it less attractive than it might have been as a place to live. The result is a retarded rate of development that has been of great concern to the managers of the factories, the administrators of the town, and its planners in the national government. From the perspective of all of these people, Ciudad Industrial has seemed a failure. Nevertheless, some of the same factors that have led to the apparent failure have also contributed directly to the development of the surrounding communities. The evidence of this development has emerged as our research has progressed, and it enables us to see the new town in a broader regional framework.

CHAPTER EIGHT

Occupations, Old and New

The most direct impact of the new town on the surrounding region has come about through the creation of new kinds of jobs. In the space of a few years, a significant proportion of the adult male populations of several communities found themselves engaged in factory work. The preceding chapter has shown how and why workers from outside came to locate in the villages. This chapter will explain how men from the villages came to occupy industrial jobs, and how the presence of new occupations has affected the local system of social stratification.

From Field to Factory

The building of Ciudad Industrial created new opportunities on a rather massive scale. Perhaps the best way to describe the initial response to these opportunities is to look at the situation in the region through the eyes of the young men during the early 1950's, since local women make up only a minute percentage of the work force. In those days, most young men in the villages lived in farming families. Many of these families held rights to land in an *ejido,* but a significant minority were landless and worked as hired hands on other people's farms. Schools had existed in many villages since the land reform in the 1930's, so most boys received some formal education, generally from one to six years of primary school. As they grew up, they became painfully aware of the decline of the *pulque* industry and of the marginality of agriculture in the region. One way or another, in school or through the mass media, they realized that these occupations carried low status. They saw their younger uncles and their older brothers leave in order to seek work in Mexico City. The creation of the new town was an event of dramatic importance: it signaled the arrival of the modern world, and promised a new and better future.

Finding a Job. During the several phases of construction of the town and the factories, Ciudad Industrial was a good source of employment for inhabitants of the region. Men from the villages streamed into the construction site seeking work. Those few with experience as masons easily found jobs. Some of the others were hired as unskilled laborers.

When the factories began to prepare for production and to employ workers, local men soon discovered that modern industry was not an automatic bonanza. The factories all involved rather sophisticated assembly lines which required highly skilled workers such as machine-tool operators and welders. Such workers were simply not be be found in the region, and had to be recruited from the national labor market. The unskilled jobs available were open to local men; but with few exceptions they went to young men, most of whom were under thirty. Educational requirements were more flexible in those days than they are now, but still a preference was shown to those with more than an average education.

We do not have precise information about the original employees of the factories, but we have excellent data about a sample of villagers, data gathered in the household survey of 1967. The sample was stratified: that is, the basic occupational groups were sampled separately to insure that the smaller groups were adequately represented. The most important groups are obviously farmers and factory workers. The first step was a complete census listing the age and occupation of every member of every household in the seven representative communities in the survey. For the sample, in the smaller villages we selected at random twenty or thirty farming households, in the larger places from forty to fifty. In all cases we interviewed the head of the household and his wife. A slightly different procedure was followed in selecting factory workers, because they are in short supply in most villages, and we wanted to interview as many as possible. The size of the samples depended again on the size of the community. In the villages with only a handful of workers, we tried to reach all of them. Some were not heads of households, but were married or unmarried sons living with parents. In the two largest communities, forty households of factory workers were selected at random. The procedure for sampling workers was also followed for other occupations, again because of the short supply in the smaller places. The major occupations of the men in the sample appear in Table 8.1

Table 8.1. Occupations of Men in the Sample of Households

	Farmers	Factory Workers	Merchants	Artisans	Others	Total
Cerro Grande	40	40	12	10	18	120
Benito Juárez	42	40	18	9	17	126
Adonde	49	7	3	1	3	63
Cristóbal	20	17	0	7	8	52
San Manuel	31	0	0	0	0	31
Santa Cecilia	36	8	1	2	1	48
Rocavista	23	2	1	3	0	28
TOTAL	241	114	35	31	47	468

At first, the facts and figures gained from the interviews might seem insignificant. If they are examined carefully, however, they yield some precise information about the process of adaptation to new economic opportunities. One aspect of that process is usually called "occupational choice." The phrase is misleading if one assumes that every individual surveys the full range of available jobs, weighs their pluses and minuses, examines his talents and training, and makes a decision. Such a description does not apply fully in the most industrialized, highly educated societies; and it is even less applicable to a developing society such as Mexico. What does occur is a sorting-out process, in which individuals are allocated to occupations by a combination of recruitment, personal decision, and sometimes accident. To understand the initial response to Ciudad Industrial, we need to understand something of that sorting-out process.

No one in our research team was present while the process was going on, so of course our understanding is limited. Nevertheless, it is possible to reconstruct some of the factors involved by looking at the survey data. I want to remind the reader that the sample includes only residents of representative villages in the valley—we did not have the resources to do an adequate survey in Ciudad Industrial itself. It would be interesting to know more about the recruitment of workers to live in the new town, but that is a separate study.

Both social research and common sense indicate that the father's occupation often influences the son's choice of career, so it is necessary to establish a control for this background variable. Cynthia Cone (1970) conducted this analysis, and she controlled for father's occupation by considering only those men in the sample who are sons of farmers. Of the 241 farmers, 175 had fathers in the same occupation; and of the 114 factory workers, 63 had fathers who were farmers.

In comparing these men of similar background, Cone found some interesting differences. All the data point to the conclusion that the farm boys who became factory workers came from the better-educated and wealthier (perhaps one should say less poverty-stricken) farming families. Their fathers had an average of 13.3 acres of land, while the fathers of men who stayed in farming had only 8.6 acres. These amounts may seem pathetically small to North Americans, but many people in Mexico support themselves on such small plots, and some survive on even less.

The household survey does not include data on the education of all the parents of the men in the sample, but we do have such information about those who are still living. They grew up during a period when little education was available in the countryside, and although their levels of education are very low, there is a great difference between the two groups. The parents of men who remained in farming had only half a year of school on the average, while those of men who became workers had one and a half years—exactly three times as much.

Educational differences among the men themselves are similar, although not as great. In looking at this variable, Cone points out that it is necessary to control for age. A straight comparison of farmers and workers in the sample would be misleading, because the farmers tend to be older, and older people had less opprotunity for education. In Table 5.2, age forty is arbitrarily taken as the cutting point between older and younger. Workers average more education than farmers, although the differences are not as great among the younger men.

Table 8.2. Age and Education of Farmers and
Factory Workers from Farm Families

	40 and Under		Over 40	
	Number	Average Years of Education	Number	Average Years of Education
Farmers	70	2.1	101	1.0
Workers	53	3.8	10	2.5

Adapted from Cone (1970).

Cone's analysis shows rather convincingly that the village men who entered the industrial labor force were not average villagers. Their parents had more land and more schooling than the average, and they themselves were better educated than their peers who continued in agriculture. From an urban point of view, they did not grow up with many advantages. But advantages are relative, and they were better prepared than others to seize the new opportunities created by industrial development.

Education was not the only advantage. After the very first years of hiring, kinship and ritual kinship ties were a valuable resource and were exploited in the search for jobs. A brother or a *compadre* already on the payroll could be useful in two ways: he was a reliable source of information about available positions, the conditions of work, skill requirements, and techniques for dealing effectively with personnel officers; he could also lobby in the interests of the job-seeker. Men with relatives in the factories had an advantage in obtaining work, and the advantage increased as the rate of expansion slowed and jobs became scarcer and harder to obtain.

I have suggested that a literal interpretation of the phrase "occupational choice" can be misleading. What happened was a process of recruitment to a role: the individual certainly made decisions along the way, but he did not necessarily make a conscious choice of a career. In the interviews, when we asked men why they took a job, the most common answers were, "By necessity" and "It was the only work available." The reality and the extent of choice depended in large part on social background: the higher the status of one's family and the better one's education, the more available opportunities there were. The whole idea of occupational choice was least appropriate for the people of lowest status. A man with no education and no land would eke out an existence as an agricultural laborer, not by choice, but because he followed the only course that he saw open to him, given his perceptions of the world and of his place in it.

Deciding Where to Live. Once a man obtained a job in the factories, he did face a clearcut decision: whether to stay in his village or move to the new town. The figures presented in the previous chapter show that the choice went overwhelmingly in favor of the villages. Why it happened this way is understandable if we examine the alternatives from the point of view of the villagers.

Ciudad Industrial offers a number of attractions. Housing is, of course, close to the factories, within easy walking distance of two of them. Every house comes with electricity, a modern bathroom, running water, and a water heater; and most of them are furnished with a bottle-gas cooking stove. All the streets are paved, and there are trees and grass forming ribbons of park between rows of houses. The schools are all new, and the teachers are better-trained than the average in the surrounding communities. The Mexican Institute of Social Security offers free health care to eligible people, and unionized factory workers are in that fortunate group. On the edge of the new town is a large clinic operated by that organization. The Saturday market offers a large variety and huge amounts of food and clothing. Every weekend, there are movies in the large theater on the main plaza. Other things could be mentioned, but this catalog is sufficient to establish the relative modernity of Ciudad Industrial.

In terms of physical facilities, the villages suffer by contrast. Most streets are muddy during the rainy season and dusty during the dry season. Only the larger places have water systems, and nowhere is water piped into every house. Electricity is more common than water systems, but it is not available in any settlement with a population less than 400. Even where it is available, there are many houses without it. Few houses have modern bathrooms, water heaters, or gas stoves, and only the town second in size to Ciudad Industrial has a large weekly market. Movies are shown several places, but never in facilities as good as those in the new town.

From the point of view of the villages, some of the differences between town and village are not as great as they might seem to outsiders. The problem of commuting to work can be solved in several ways. Some men in the closest settlements ride bicycles. The factories have regular bus routes for picking up workers, and private service is frequent. The more highly paid workers are beginning to acquire automobiles, and three cars at an intersection constitute a traffic jam. The houses in Ciudad Industrial may have modern facilities; yet all but the most expensive are very small. They are unsuitable for extended families, and there is no way to obtain a house next door or down the street for elderly parents or other relatives. The past twenty years have seen a huge investment in public education in Mexico. Only the smallest villages in the region have no schools; and in those cases, there is usually one nearby. For years villagers have been accustomed to going to weekly market in Los Llanos or some other town. Hardly anyone would consider moving his residence to the new town just to be close to a market.

In comparing the new town with the surrounding communities, the inhabitants of the latter pay more attention to the quality of life and of human relationships than to the physical amenities, such as they are. They describe life in Ciudad Industrial as cold and relationships as distant. The general sterility and monotony of the design reinforces the perception of coldness; and relationships certainly are distant compared to the intimacy of small communities and extended families. The population is drawn from throughout the country, and many people continue to maintain an identification with the home community through visits and other communications as well as through bonds of affection. Ciudad Industrial has numerous organizations such as "Automotive Workers from San Pablo, State of Tlaxcala," that is, men from the same town who work in the same plant. These organizations sponsor special events at religious fiestas, social occasions, and other activities. In December 1966, the Automotive Workers from San Pablo sponsored the most impressive feature of the fiesta for the Virgin of Guadalupe, the patron saint of Mexico (Wolf 1958). That feature was a large sand painting of the Virgin placed on the steps of the church. It was executed by a rather well known painter who had been born in San Pablo and who had exhibited, among many other places, at the United Nations in New York City. By maintaining social relationships and emotional ties with home towns and villages, these kinds of organizations retard the emergence of a sense of community in Ciudad Industrial.

The sense of coldness and distance is also emphasized by the absence or scarcity of normal gathering places, such as shops, small restaurants, and especially saloons. In Mexican towns, houses are generally built immediately adjacent to the sidewalks, and dozens of front rooms contain stores that sell food and sundries. The classical saloon—boisterous, full of cigarette smoke and the pungent aroma of tequila, and limited to men—is one of the chief centers of male social activity. Both saloons and front-room shops are strictly prohibited by the administration of the new town. In an ordinary town of 12,000 there would be a great diversity of small restaurants, in many of which the simplicity of the decor carries no hint of the excellence of the cuisine. Ciudad Industrial requires the licensing of all restaurants, and there are only three, none of which attains the culinary level of the establishments in nearby Cerro Grande.

In short, the new town gains an urban appearance from its utilities, streets, houses, and public buildings; but it lacks urban facilities for social life and recreation.

The vast majority of village men who took jobs in the factories saw the situation as I have described it. They chose to maintain residence in their natal communities, where they could keep the social ties that were important to them and live in an atmosphere that appeared more "natural" than that in the new town. Where factory workers chose to live may not seem very significant in itself, but in this case it had important implications for trends of change. These men were the first, and remain the only, villagers to work in a fully "modern" setting—a factory with an impersonal assembly line producing complex machinery—and with an entire operation organized by a bureaucracy oriented to national goals of industrialization and development. The workers receive a steady stream of messages—some from the foreman, some from fellow workers, and some almost by osmosis—urging or nudging them to embrace the values and goals of modern Mexico. These goals are the goals of the present phase of the Revolution: a higher level of education for all, and both national and personal progress through economic development. The workers carry these values home and communicate them to their peers in agriculture and commerce. They reinforce, on an immediate and personal level, the schools and the mass media.

Changing Patterns of Stratification

Occupations do not exist in a vacuum; they are an essential element in the system of social stratification. For example, tapping the *maguey* plants in the days of the great haciendas was not just a way for uneducated rural men to make their meager livings; it was the basis, in human labor, of an elaborate social hierarchy.

The land reform of the Revolution freed the peasants and the *maguey* tappers from bondage to the hacienda system, but it did not change their position in the national class structure. Neither did the coming of the new town change their position; but it did create new opportunities for them to move out of that status, and it channeled factory workers from outside the region into the villages. The occupational mix in some of the villages changed greatly and produced modifications in the local stratification system.

The Distribution of Wealth. One dimension of the stratification system is the uneven distribution of wealth. Since the definition of economic levels is arbitrary in any society, I do not want to define precise ranges of income. Instead, I shall describe the life styles of three families which represent the great differences present in the villages and then the significance of the differences will be discussed after the facts are presented.

Pulque tappers and other landless agricultural laborers have been, and still are, at the bottom of the economic scale. In fact, their relative position has deteriorated as other groups have benefitted from industrialization. In a developing society one must run hard to stay even, and these groups have not been able to run very fast. In material terms, their lives seem severely impoverished by North American standards. Emilio García, a *pulque* tapper in Cerro Grande, lives with his wife, four sons, and two daughters-in-law in a one-room house with a dirt floor. His income of $4.80 a week is small but reliable, since he works for one of the wealthy families in the community. His relationship to his employer is a good example of the persistence of the kind of patron-client relationship that was common on the haciendas before the Revolution. The "client" depends on the "patron" for whatever security he and his family possess; in return he offers unquestioning loyalty and patient deference.

The García house has only one small window, and candles furnish the only illumination at night. The members of the family sleep on the floor on *petates* "reed mats." There are a few low stools, but no chairs or tables, and certainly no modern appliances. On an ordinary day breakfast consists of tea, tortillas, and the typical hot sauce made from green tomatoes, chili peppers, and onions. The big meal of the day in Mexico is taken in the early afternoon, when this family usually eats clear soup, beans, tortillas, and *pulque.* In the evening there is no supper, only tea to drink. In adequate quantities this diet, simple as it is, will not lead to malnutrition; corn is a nourishing food, and tortillas also furnish minerals, since the corn is soaked in lime to soften it for grinding. Beans are the source of proteins, and hot sauce and *pulque* are rich in vitamins. Still, to say the least, the diet is austere.

In the survey we included a check list of ten "modern" appliances, with an iron heated by glowing charcoal as the least modern and the least expensive, and a television as the most. The Garcías have none of these items. By comparison, 81 percent of the households in the sample have radios, and 41 percent have electric irons. Señora García considers her pottery dishes to be the most valuable possession of the household. And since there is no running water, she carries water from a public fountain along with many other women in Cerro Grande. The house lacks even a latrine; a corner of the compound, or a nearby field, serves instead.

The middle range of wealth in the villages is represented by successful farmers, small businessmen, and skilled workers in the factories. The range of income and life style is wide, and no one family can represent it adequately. Many factory workers have larger and more reliable incomes than most shopkeepers; but, since they tend to be younger, their standard of living is not necessarily higher. Take for example the family of a factory worker in Cerro Grande: José Moreno, an assembly-line worker in the car and truck factory, has a weekly income of $25.40. It may seem like a pittance to North Americans, but in Mexico it is a respectable figure. He, his wife, and six children ranging in age from three to twelve, live in a six-room house with a simple tile floor. It is lighted by electricity, and all members of the family sleep in beds with mattresses. The house is furnished with wooden tables, chairs, and cabinets, but no upholstered furniture.

The diet is notably better than that of the *pulque* tapper. For breakfast there are eggs, bread, and hot chocolate. The large mid-day meal consists of soup, meat, beans, fresh vegetables, and soft drinks. For supper the family eats beans, bread, and milk.

Water is piped into the house from a private cistern, and there is a latrine in the back. The Moreno family owns an electric iron, a blender, a sewing machine, and a record player. Strangely enough, there is no radio, although most people at this income level own one. The item of greatest value in the house is the bottle-gas stove in the kitchen.

At the top of the economic scale in the villages are a few "wealthy" farmers and businessmen, and a very few middle-level factory executives. In terms of the national class system, all of these people would be considered middle-class; their relative wealth in the local context would appear insignificant in Mexico City or in many provincial cities.

Gonzalo Sánchez, a businessman in Benito Juárez, has a standard of living that is exceeded by only a handful of people outside of Ciudad Industrial and Los Llanos, the commercial center. From a store and public baths, he reports an income that averages $73.00 a week. He and his family (his wife and five children) have a substantial house with all of the amenities of the Morenos, and many more. City water is piped into the house, and there is a bathroom with running water.

The diet is not so different from that of the Morenos, except that it frequently includes meat for breakfast, and greater variety at the main meal of the day.

The family is one of the few that owns a television, and it has all of the modern applicances on the check-list except a record player and refrigerator. More impressively, there is a piano, which is considered by Señora Sánchez to be the possession of greatest value. There are also a car and a truck, both 1952 models, a vintage that is more common in Mexico than in the United States.

The variation in level of living is summarized in Table 8.3. The three families described here represent conditions of life that could be described, from the point of view of village standards, as "poverty," "relative comfort," and "affluence." It would be misleading to describe them as lower, middle and upper classes, since the upper level in a village is likely to be squarely middle class in national terms.

Table 8.3. The Standard of Living of Individual Families at Three Social Levels

	Pulque Tapper	Factory Worker	"Wealthy" Businessman
Weekly income (head of household)	$4.80	$25.40	$73.00
Size of house	1 room	6 rooms	6 rooms
Floor	Dirt	Tile	Tile
Lighting	Candles	Electric light	Electric light
Sleeping arrangements	Reed mats on floor	Beds with mattresses	Beds with mattresses
Source of water	Public fountain	Piped from own cistern	Piped from town reservoir
Article of greatest value	Pottery dishes	Gas stove	Piano

The Distribution of Prestige. Prestige, as well as wealth, is distributed unevenly in all societies. This dimension has been investigated intensively by Barbara Simon (1968, 1972) as part of her comprehensive study of social stratification in Benito Juárez. Preliminary work revealed that informants systematically ranked their fellow villagers in terms of what they called *categoría*, which corresponds to our notion of prestige. Simon selected eight informants who were widely acquainted with the people in the village and who represented the major occupational groups. She gave them 160 cards, each with the name of a married couple, and asked them to arrange the cards from high to low according to degree of *categoría*. She was careful not to suggest whether the informants should arrange the names in a continuum or in distinct groups.

Six of the informants sorted their fellow villagers into the four groups, ranked from high to low, which appear in Table 8.4. The other two informants formed six levels, but the top two and the bottom two correspond to the upper and lower groups in the table.

Table 8.4. The Distribution of Prestige in Benito Juárez

A.	Top merchants
	Professionals
	Managers and administrators
	Successful farmers who participate in public affairs
B.	White collar workers
	Middle-level merchants
	Successful farmers and cattle dealers who are not prominent in public affairs
C.	Factory workers
	Railroad workers
D.	Farmers who are also proprietors of small shops
	Artisans and farmers who work their own *ejido* parcels
	Landless agricultural workers

Adapted from Simon (1968:30)

There was also a high degree of agreement about the placement of specific individuals in groups. The disagreements concerned cases of mistaken identity or individuals in a transitional position between two levels.

The degree of consensus about prestige that Simon has found is impressive, even startling, especially in view of the tremendous changes that have occurred in Benito Juárez over the past forty years. The consensus is evidence of the psychological and cultural reality of the notion of prestige, which has been difficult to measure or to define precisely, but of which the people of Benito Juárez—or at least Simon's informants—have a clear conception. They seem universally to rank their fellow citizens according to their occupations.

The distribution of prestige in Benito Juárez shows considerable persistence of the traditional Latin American pattern. In a paper written twenty years ago but still widely read, Beals (1953:338) emphasized the great gaps in Latin American society between manual laborers and people in all other kinds of work. The traditional culture did not recognize the possibility that craftsmen or skilled workers might be included in the middle class if they achieved a similar standard of living and adopted a comparable system of values. According to Beals (1953:338), twenty years ago there was "no real break in the fundamental distinction between those who work with their hands and those who do not." Even though factory workers are rather well paid, they still have relatively little prestige. On the other hand, the division between those who work with their hands and those who do not is not as distinct as it once was, at least not in Mexico. With the process of modernization, levels of income, education, and the sophistication of industrial labor have all increased, and the traditional middle-class sense of superiority has become increasingly difficult to maintain.

The place of the farmers in the system of prestige represents another complication. "Ordinary" farmers are in the bottom group, but "successful" farmers are placed in one of the top two levels, depending on whether they participate in public affairs. Why do some farmers enjoy high prestige? After all, no matter how many people they hire, they do some work with their hands. The answer involves two considerations. In the first place, the successful farmers are the larger operators. Because land is owned communally, they do not *own* more land, but in one way or another they control more; and control over land, the traditional source of wealth, brings prestige. In the second place, these farmers are successful in essentially the same way that top merchants are: they have been able to manipulate available resources to serve their own ends. Therefore they are lumped with businessmen in the system of prestige.

Community and Nation. The results of Simon's research in Benito Juárez fit reasonably well into the national scheme of social classes (see Chapter 6), but some qualifications are necessary. For example, no one in Benito Juárez would be considered upper class in national terms; a community so small is not likely to have people at that level. At the other extreme, Level D corresponds to González Cosío's definition of the popular class. The problem comes with Levels A, B, and C in Benito Juárez. In the national scheme the people in these levels would all be middle class; but locally the top merchants in Level A would not accept the factory workers of Level C as members of the same class. Perhaps the most reasonable way of reconciling the differences is to apply the point of view that I stated in Chapter 6. That point of view recognizes that social classes in industrial societies cannot be rigidly defined. How the investigator groups people into classes depends on what criteria he adopts, and on the fact that different criteria are useful for different purposes. Merchants and factory workers certainly share no feelings of class solidarity; but with burgeoning industrialization, skilled workers are increasingly coming to share values and skills that can be considered middle class.

In the towns and villages around Ciudad Industrial, one of the most important developments is the growth of the broadly defined middle sector which includes skilled workers, white collar employees, and merchants. The same change is taking place throughout the rest of Mexico, although it seldom occurs in communities so small. Part of the significance of this growth is economic: higher incomes create a larger internal market for the products of Mexican industry, which in turn stimulates further industrialization. At least as important are the cultural changes involved in this growth of the middle sector. Most of its members embrace an ideology of modernization which stands in sharp contrast to the stereotype of Mexican fatalism and the attitude that Foster has called the "image of the limited good." That picture of Mexico may still apply in some villages and in some areas, but in the Valley of Los Llanos it has increasingly given way to a set of ideas that might be called the modern mode of thought.

These ideas are all grounded in the tradition that was created by the intellectuals of the Revolution, discussed briefly in Chapter 2. First, there is a sense of nationalism, a proud identification with the nation as an object of personal allegiance. This nationalism contrasts with the pre-Revolutionary emphasis on loyalty to the village, the region, or, in the case of the many Indian groups, the culture. Local and regional pride is still strong, and is one of the features of Mexico that appeals to North Americans. But it is supplemented more and more by a strong national allegiance.

The modern mode of thought also includes a belief in the need for rapid economic and social development, designed to make Mexico a modern nation with a rising standard of living. One specific goal is to narrow the economic gap between Mexico and the colossus to the north. A surprising number of Mexicans have worked in the United States or visited relatives there, and others have an image of the "good life" based on the movies and television. Uneducated agricultural laborers often have a lively sense of the need to catch up with the United States; and, among the better educated classes, factory workers and white collar employees sometimes express with considerable eloquence a rather sophisticated ideology of development.

A commitment to education is a third feature of the new thought, for education is seen as the means to both personal and national advancement. A new school building in a village is a symbol of progress that is valued by many of the residents. Parents with little or no education sometimes have extremely high aspirations for their children, hoping that they will complete secondary school and perhaps even acquire professional training. A strong faith in education has been produced by the traditional respect for educated people, based on the pre-Revolutionary class system, and a new appreciation of the power of knowledge.

In the United States, this modern faith in learning seems to be giving way to a postmodern disillusionment; but in Mexico the faith is still growing. The effects of that faith form the subject of the next chapter.

CHAPTER NINE

Education:
Aspirations and Realities

In Mexico, schools are a national concern of high priority; and in the Valley of Los Llanos, education is crucial to the adaptive strategies of individuals. The Revolution's goal of universal schooling has still not been attained; but great progress has been made, especially during the past fifty years. Formal instruction was first extended to many rural areas by the Cultural Missions which began operating in the early 1920's. They consisted of teams of specialists who traveled around a circuit of villages and who served as teachers, social workers, and promoters of community development. The next major effort was devoted to the construction and staffing of schools in the agrarian communities that were established as part of the land reform of 1934-40. These programs were merely the beginning of a huge national investment in education. Today the traveler can observe thousands of new or expanded schools in all of the larger cities and in some of the smallest villages. The increasingly industrialized society needs trained personnel, and one of the world's highest rates of demographic growth produces large numbers of potential personnel to be trained.

In the region of Los Llanos every school but one was established during the Revolutionary years (Roufs 1971:142). The first was a private primary school founded in the town of Los Llanos in 1911, after the beginning of the Revolution but not connected with it. The next school in the region, also in Los Llanos and built in 1924, was publicly supported. Then in the 1930's many elementary schools were established. By 1967 nineteen of the twenty-two communities in the network had schools, although only six were full primary schools with six grades. The area's first secondary school was built in Los Llanos in 1951. The biggest spurt in the investment in local education came with the building of the new town; it has one secondary school and three primary schools, one of which is private.

The Mission of the Schools

In every part of Mexico, even in remote Indian villages, public education has been the principal means for building a wide popular base for nationalist ideology. From the first year, the schools teach Mexican geography, Mexican history, and the lives of Mexican heroes. The crises and accomplishments of the nation are represented by such men as Benito Juárez, the Zapotec Indian who became a reform President in the last century, and Emiliano Zapata, the agrarian leader in the Revolution. The schools are the foci of many civic rituals, and the teachers organize local celebrations of all important national holidays. There are pageants and parades by pupils and speeches by principals and teachers, offered in honor of national heroes, but also serving as symbolic statements of national unity and continuing commitment to the goals of the Revolution.

Anthropological research has not adequately conveyed the growing importance of education in Mexican villages, partly because most of the best-known studies were conducted before the recent boom in school construction. In the towns and villages around Ciudad Industrial, especially in the smaller places, the school is displacing the church as the center of many activities. If a village is large enough to have a school, it usually faces the plaza; in Benito Juárez, for example, the school is on the plaza although the new church is not.

When the residents of the Los Llanos region contemplate their future, they see education as perhaps the most crucial resource. It is the means to a better job than one's father had, and a better job represents escape from the limitations of a life in marginal agriculture.

The belief in education is not naive; years of schooling are valuable in the job market both in the new town and elsewhere in the nation. Over the years, the factories in Ciudad Industrial have raised considerably the educational levels for skilled jobs and for apprenticeships for such positions. When the factories began operating in 1955, the better educated applicants had better chances for jobs, but there were no minimal educational levels for most positions. Schensul (1972) reports that by 1965, a primary school certificate became the minimum requirement for employment in the factories, and today preference is shown to those with one or more years of secondary school.

The Mexican system includes six years of primary school, three years of secondary, and three more years of preparatory school for those with the talent and resources to proceed to a university or to professional training. The system is highly centralized with most public schools supported principally by the federal government, which pays teachers' salaries and some of the cost of constructing the buildings. In spite of the centralization, much local effort is devoted to education. The community must contribute both labor for construction and some money for new buildings. Since the school is seen as a significant resource, local political leaders participate in educational affairs. In writing about villages in the Valley of Los Llanos, Mundale (1971:205) reports that:

> . . . the schools are the nation's clearest voice in the community. . . It is not surprising, then, that the municipal president makes a point of being involved in school matters. He assists with raising money and organizing work crews; he visits state and federal agencies; and he participates centrally in the dedication of new buildings.

A new school of simple, modern design, overlooking the village plaza, symbolizes the political and social importance of education.

Aspirations

If the extended availability of schooling has been impressive, the rise in aspirations has been spectacular. The villager of the Los Llanos region no longer lives in a narrow world, fatalistically resigned to a hard life. His horizons have been extended by schools, the mass media, and travel to urban centers or contact with relatives who have traveled. He has seen the benefits and comforts of modern technology, and he does not worry about its ill effects. In order to share those benefits, he realizes that he needs a well-paying job in the modern sector of the economy, and that to obtain such a job he needs a high level of education. The result of this thought process applied to a large number of individuals is a level of aspiration far beyond that which the system can satisfy.

The commitment to education does not mean, of course, that there is equality of access or uniformity of attitudes. Some variation in the region is represented by the three families described in the preceding chapter. Emilio García, the 48-year-old *pulque* tapper, has never been to school, although his wife has had two years of education. Such lack of schooling is not uncommon among people of their generation; but it is unusual that their four sons, ranging in age from six to thirty, have never been to school. In the survey of households, we asked both husbands and wives about their aspirations for the education and occupations of both their sons and daughters, assuming that the aspirations for daughters might be considerably different in a society where the role of women still involves many constraints. Although none of the children has been to school, Señor García would have liked the children of both sexes to have had a grade school education and a job in the world of commerce, which he sees as more rewarding than agricultural work. His wife did not reach even these modest aspirations: she would have hoped for only four years of school and a job in agriculture.

In the middle-income family of José Moreno, a 39-year-old factory worker, the husband has four years of school and the wife five. Their oldest child, a boy of twelve, has already begun secondary school. They agree with each other about their hopes for their children: careers in engineering for the sons, and as beauticians for the daughters, with the appropriate educational preparation.

Gonzalo Sánchez, representing the local upper-income level, is a 50-year-old businessman. Since neither he nor his wife answered when asked their level of education, a likely assumption is that they have had little schooling and did not care to reveal the fact. Whether or not this is the case, we do know that their children are making good progress in the educational system. In 1967 the youngest child was still in primary school and preparing to go on. Another was in secondary school, and a son and a daughter were in preparatory school. The oldest child, a girl of 21, was studying to become an accountant. The aspirations that the Sánchezes hold for their children are appropriate to their present and potential educational attainments. Both parents would like their sons to be engineers. Señor Sánchez would like the daughters to follow careers in business, and the oldest is heading in that direction. Señora Sanchez would like her daughters to be bilingual secretaries—a prestigious job in Mexico.

Among these three families, the Morenos and the Sánchezes are representative of their occupational group. Factory workers and merchants are highly likely to want their children, especially their sons, to have professional or technical occupations. Emilio García is only partly typical of farmers, most of whom desire primary educations for their children, as he does, but who also prefer that their sons be factory workers instead of merchants.

The high aspirations among the people in the Valley of Los Llanos and the similarities and differences among occupational groups can be demonstrated most convincingly by looking at the survey data. Since education is almost universally perceived as the principle means to a better job, occupational aspirations are shown to be more fundamental than educational aspirations.

In his extensive analysis of the data, John J. Poggie (1968, 1972) points out that, since aspirations are higher among the younger and the better educated in all occupational groups, a comparison of occupations requires a control for these background variables of age and education. Farmers and factory workers are the most important groups and the only ones with enough members to allow for such control. Factory workers are younger and better educated than farmers, and their higher aspirations might arise from those factors, not from occupation. However, Table 6.1 shows that this is not the case. When subgroups of similar age and education are compared, factory workers still have much higher aspirations for their sons' occupations. For example, among men with two to four years

Table 9.1. Aspirations for Sons' Occupations

Occupation desired for sons	Workers (15-49 years)		Younger farmers (15-49 years)		Older farmers (50 years and older)	
Educational level 0-1 years						
Farmer	0	0.0%	2	4.9%	12	22.2%
Worker	3	25.0%	21	51.2%	22	40.7%
Technical and professional	5	41.7%	7	17.1%	6	11.1%
Other	2	16.6%	8	19.5%	9	16.7%
No answer	2	16.6%	3	7.3%	5	9.3%
Subtotals	12	99.9%	41	100.0%	54	100.0%
Educational level 2-4 years						
Farmer	0	0.0%	4	5.5%	2	15.4%
Worker	15	32.6%	26	47.3%	6	46.2%
Technical and professional	24	52.2%	13	23.6%	2	15.4%
Other	7	15.2%	11	20.0%	2	15.4%
No answer	0	0.0%	2	3.6%	1	7.6%
Subtotals	46	100.0%	55	100.0%	13	100.0%
Educational level 5 years or more						
Farmer	0	0.0%	1	11.1%	0	0.0%
Worker	5	13.5%	5	55.6%	1	100.0%
Technical and professional	30	81.0%	2	22.2%	0	0.0%
Other	2	5.4%	0	0.0%	0	0.0%
No answer	0	0.0%	1	11.1%	0	0.0%
Subtotals	37	99.9%	9	100.0%	1	100.0%
TOTALS	95		105		68	

From Poggie (1968:170)

of school, 52.2 percent of the workers desire technical or professional jobs for their sons, whereas only 23.6 percent of the farmers in the same age range, and only 15.4 percent of the older farmers, have equal aspirations.

The two most striking results in the table are the strong rejection of farming by farmers, especially the younger ones, and the high aspirations of both farmers and factory workers, especially the better educated ones. Altogether only twenty farmers (12 percent of that group) want their sons to follow the same vocation, only six (5 percent) of the younger farmers do, and not one of the workers would like to see his sons in farming. Almost half of the farmers at all levels of education want their sons to be factory workers; and among the workers with five or more years of education, an amazing 81 percent desire technical or professional jobs for their sons. Educational aspirations are consistent with these results: in general, farmers hope that their sons will at least finish grade school; and workers hope for technical or professional training.

Realities

What are the chances for sons to fulfill the high aspirations that their fathers hold for them? Since many of the sons are not yet adults, it is impossible to say conclusively. But the statistics on those who finish school are far from encouraging. In the United States it is customary to discuss drop-out rates, but that terminology is misleading with regard to Mexico. When a student leaves school it is not usually because he chooses to drop-out; he does so most often because of a lack of opportunities in the system or a scarcity of family resources. Of the communities represented in the survey of households, only Benito Juárez and Cerro Grande have full primary schools, and these are also the towns with large numbers of factory workers. Table 9.2 shows rather dramatically what happens to every 100

Table 9.2. School Completion Rates

	Benito Juárez[1]	Cerro Grande[2]
Start primary school	100	100
Complete primary school	75	55
Start secondary school	15	15
Complete high school	3 (estimate)	No Data

[1] Schensul 1972:24-8.
[2] Roufs 1971:146-7.

students who start grade school. These days, and in town centers such as these, almost all of the children start school; but if only 3 percent finish high school, there is no way that the hopes of their fathers can be fulfilled. When it is difficult to find a place in a secondary school and to pay the costs of living away from home, the chances of a technical or professional career are slim indeed.

The aspirations of young people for themselves seem to be even higher than their fathers' hopes for them. We do not have precise comparisons, because we did not interview any students in our household survey. But we do have extensive data, collected and analyzed by Timothy Roufs (1971), on the aspirations of all students in the last year of primary schools in the research region. Roufs administered questionnaires, not to a sample, but to all students in these classes. They are, as we have seen, a select group; they are the ones who have survived in school. Still, they are not yet highly selected, since they represent from 50 percent to 75 percent of the age group in towns and villages, and almost 100 percent in the new town, where the grade school drop-out rate is very low. Table 9.3 presents a few highlights of Roufs' data. The primary schools in

Table 9.3. Occupational Choice of Male Students
In Sixth Grade

	Percentage From Farm Families	Occupational Choice		
Community		Farmer	Factory Worker	Professional
Ciudad Industrial	10.0%	0.8%	6.7%	60.5%
Los Llanos	34.7%	3.0%	23.2%	35.4%
Cerro Grande	21.3%	0	19.7%	27.9%
Benito Juárez	42.9%	0	72.0%	20.0%
Malapan	41.2%	0	21.1%	0
Serena	54.5%	0	85.7%	0
Aguarico	44.5%	0	25.0%	37.5%

Adapted from Roufs (1971:157, 174). Percentages of choice do not total 100% because all choices are not included in this simplified table.

the larger places, especially in the new town, draw some students from surrounding areas. Ciudad Industrial has no resident farmers, but 10 percent of the sixth graders come from farm families. The figures speak for themselves: only five (3.8 percent) sixth grade boys want to be farmers. Most of them aspire to be factory workers or professionals, although few of them will have an opportunity to finish high school, and job openings in local factories are scarce.

Further evidence of the discrepancy between aspirations and reality is reported by Schensul (1972). Among the 1970 graduating class of the primary school in Benito Juárez, her interviews confirm the students' overwhelming preference for factory or professional careers. These kinds of jobs require at least a high school education; but, as Table 9.2 shows, only one-fifth of those who complete primary school are able to go on to secondary school. In turn, the estimate is that only one-fifth of those who start secondary school will finish. Schensul found that, among the grade school graduates who were unable to continue their education, a few sons of factory workers found places as apprentices in the plants where their fathers work. Others found temporary employment as errand boys or the like, and still others started commuting regularly to Ciudad Industrial, where they would wait in front of the union offices and hope, usually in vain, that their names would be called for a day's labor in one of the factories.

The problem is not that education has been a failure; as a matter of fact, it has succeeded all too well. People have come to see education as the principal resource in the struggle for personal advancement and social progress. Through it they have come to expect more than the system can deliver.

CHAPTER TEN

Adaptive Strategies and the Problems of the Future

The Valley of Los Llanos is almost an exact miniature of Mexican society. It contained some of the classic haciendas in the days when that social system dominated the countryside. The scenarios of the Revolution—land reform, education, and industrialization—were acted out in the towns and villages of the region, and today a new town representing a large investment of the nation's capital dominates the scene. A study of the region is useful in several ways: it can help us to understand how individuals have adapted to the sometimes cataclysmic changes in their lives; it can demonstrate the interplay between the planned and unplanned effects of a major project of directed change; and it can serve as a way of comprehending some of the workings of modern Mexican society and the directions in which it is heading.

The Treadmill of Modernization

Modernization in the Valley of Los Llanos seems to run on a treadmill. The Revolution brought schools to counter ignorance and then factories to combat unemployment. The schools prepared increasing numbers of the young to participate in modern society and, with the mass media, they encouraged higher and higher levels of aspiration. The schools emphasized national identity and the goals of economic development, while the mass media conveyed vividly the material benefits of

133

modern technology, which had seemed remote indeeed to people living in poverty and isolation. The factories gave jobs to young men from the villages, jobs that were well paid by local standards. They also attracted many skilled workers and their young families, some of whom settled in the villages. Both local and outside workers became envoys for modern thought, thereby adding direct personal influence to the messages communicated through education and the mass media.

But at the same time other trends were developing to overwhelm the gains. Within ten years after construction, the factories ceased to expand. And since the factories were new, the work force was young: in the sample for the survey in 1967, almost all the employees were under 40, and no one was over 50. Meanwhile, the rate of population growth, both locally and nationally, remained one of the highest in the world, so that, for every villager who obtained a job in Ciudad Industrial, there are now three or four young men looking for similar work. But no one is ready to retire, and few jobs are available.

The imbalance created by a growing population and a stable market for labor is nowhere more apparent than in Ciudad Industrial itself. There the population is young, and the birth rate is especially high. The children who were born in the town's early years are now entering the labor force, and their numbers will increase in the future. Although they have had more opportunities for a better education than did the young people in the villages, it does them no good to be better qualified for jobs that do not exist.

Adaptive Strategies

A strategy is a plan that is continually modified in the light of changing circumstances. It can be extended to include a course of adaptive behavior, all aspects of which are not necessarily results of conscious planning. The way in which an individual copes with changing circumstances depends on his perceptions of the world, his personal resources, and the way he is able to draw upon the social resources available to him.

Perceptions of the world are shaped by cultural heritage. An excellent example of this process is George Foster's analysis of the "image of limited good," which he sees as a basic assumption in the culture of the Mexican community of Tzintzuntzan. It shapes the inhabitants' perception of both the world and the opportunities in it; or rather, in their case, the lack of opportunities in it. These perceptions in turn influence the people's attempts to cope with their situation as they see fit.

If the inhabitants of the Valley of Los Llanos ever held an "image of limited good," they have given it up with a vengeance; and they may regret their reversal. The advent of modern technology, in the form of the factories and the new town, and the messages of the mass media, demonstrated to their satisfaction that certain kinds of goods—consumer goods, jobs, and knowledge, for example—were not limited. On the contrary, they seemed to be rapidly expandable. But there is another side of the coin: because of changes in the national economy, the expansion may grind to a halt as rapidly as it began. That is exactly what has happened in the Valley of Los Llanos: just as many of the people were beginning to embrace a faith in continual progress based on modern technology, progress reached a plateau. The "good things of life" were proven to be limited after all, especially when the population was growing rapidly. In the traditional Mexican village, fatalism and pessimism provided convenient adaptations to the real scarcity of opportunities. Industrialization opened up opportunities, but not fast enough to keep up with rising expectations. So again there is the problem of bringing perceptions in line with comtemporary social reality.

Personal resources are another element on which strategies are based. They include readily measurable things, such as money, and more elusive things, such as experience. The increasing specialization of work that accompanies industrialization places growing emphasis on formal credentials. Although education is the principal currency in the market place of credentials, certain kinds of jobs require more specialized demonstrations of aptitude.

A stratified society—even one such as Mexico that allows increasing opportunities for social mobility—is characterized by unequal distribution of resources. In the Valley of Los Llanos, the offspring of factory employees and of the wealthier merchants enter the world with certain advantages over the children of most of the agricultural people. The families of the former have higher-than-average incomes, their parents tend to have more than the usual amount of education, and they have higher aspirations for their children. Largely for these reasons, the offspring are likely to acquire more educaton, which then gives them an advantage in the job market. Obtaining the more desirable jobs further consolidates their position in the system of stratification.

Social resources are also distributed unevenly. By social resources I mean those kinds of personal bonds and group ties on which an individual can draw in order to further his own ends. This way of looking at social structure rejects the view that it pulls the strings while the participants dance like puppets. On the contrary, social relationships are capital to be saved, invested, or used up as required; ties of kinship or *compadrazgo* are a crucial resource, without which it is virtually impossible to obtain a job in the factories in Ciudad Industrial. Here also the offspring of factory employees have a great advantage over other young people.

An individual with a certain perception of the world draws on the available resources to fashion a means of coping. It would be impossible to discuss all of the possible strategies; instead I would like to summarize the principal ones and to consider their future relevance.

The Patron-Client Strategy. Before the Revolution, attachment to the wealthy owner of a hacienda was the single most common means of survival. The client offered cheap labor, loyalty, and deference; in return he and his family received a degree of security and a sense of belonging to an important social unit with a glorious past and a guaranteed future. Although by undermining the wealth of the estate-owning class, the land reform greatly reduced the availability of this mode of survival, it did not entirely eliminate it. The life of Emilio García, described in Chapters 8 and 9, is testimony to the continuing possibility of patron-client relationships.

Patron-client relationships seem to be an enduring aspect of Mexican culture. Since they carry some advantages for everyone concerned, they will probably persist in those segments of society that are insulated from the influences of industrialization and bureaucracy. However, since these segments of society will continue to decrease, the patron-client strategy will be viable for fewer and fewer people as the years go by. It will continue to be a useful adaptation for people who prize highly personalized social ties, but it will be increasingly identified with the traditional sector of society.

Pulque. Possibilities in agriculture are constrained by the national market, by local resources in land and water, by the available technology, and by the supply of laborers with appropriate skills. For the production of *pulque,* local resources are ample, since the *maguey* requires only rocky hillsides and little water. Except for the mode of transportation, technology has remained unchanged for centuries. It is what economists call a "labor-intensive" technology; that is, it requires large amounts of human effort and relatively little capital investment. Since the Valley of Los Llanos is one of the traditional centers of *pulque* production, the supply of labor with the required rudimentary skills is more than ample. Therefore, the only constraint is the state of the market, which has been declining for several decades. Because of the symbolic importance of *pulque* as a typical regional beverage, I would not be so rash as to predict its disappearance. But there is every reason to expect that the contraction of the market will continue, as Mexico becomes more and more modern, and as a larger segment of the population acquires a taste for beer and soft drinks.

The decline of the *pulque* business has meant a reduction in the number of people who make part or all of their living from it. Of the 475 men interviewed in the survey of households, only 13 work full time as *pulque* tappers. These figures apply only to the kinds of communities represented in the sample: the head towns and the larger villages. A slightly higher proportion of the total male labor force in the region is involved with *maguey,* because the hilly flanks of the valleys contain a number of ex-haciendas which still specialize in *pulque,* and which furnish a supplemental income for some people. The family of Alfonso Velasco in Cerro Grande, described in Chapter 6 as an example of an extended family compound, owns a total of more than 5,000 *maguey* plants. A tapper works the plants and gives the family a share of the proceeds.

These pockets of specialization are all that remain of the industry that once dominated the valley. Unless major new uses are found for the *maguey,* it will furnish possibilities of survival for fewer and fewer people in the future.

Barley. While the *pulque* industry is limited by the market, the barley business is constrained by resources and technology. Rainfall is too unreliable to guarantee a good crop every year. Although additional technology, especially in the form of small-scale irrigation, could improve yields, the valley floor lies at a high altitude, and the surrounding terrain does not offer many possibilities for water reservoirs. The switch from *maguey* to barley was a good strategy in the past, but it has gone as far as it can go with the present level of capital investment. In fact, the adaptive potential of almost any form of agriculture in the Valley of Los Llanos cannot be increased without technological changes that are highly unlikely to occur in the near future.

Factory Work. The factories in Ciudad Industrial were constructed, in part, to create jobs in a depressed region. No doubt because some of the goals were matters of social welfare, private enterprise was not involved in the project. The publicly-owned firms that located there required mainly skilled workers who had to be imported. With their relatively high incomes and spending power, they have been an economic boon for the area. The local men who obtained jobs in industry began, almost without exception, at the lowest levels of skill and salary. Some of them, with on-the-job training furnished by the factories, have been able to work their way into better jobs.

One of the most successful is Raul Velasco, one of the sons of the man from Cerro Grande. He started as a riverter's helper in the railroad car construction company, but after several years he became a welder's apprentice. Soon he will be a full-fledged welder, and his ability to hold a more responsible position is indicated by the fact that he has worked up to the position of secretary of his union. Velasco's commitment to modernization and advancement is further demonstrated by his union activity and by his efforts to learn English. While in school he began to acquire some knowledge of English, a skill which is widely regarded as the gateway to advancement. Later he was one of the most diligent students in the evening English classes taught by some of the field workers associated with our research project.

Velasco's career represents the opposite of the patron-client strategy. Even within an industrial and bureaucratic context, the quality of personal relationships with supervisors and fellow workers is important. But the nature of the interaction within the industrial environment is very different from the kind that characterizes patron-client ties. The traditional deference and submissiveness are unpalatable to Velasco: he interacts with superiors with an air of confidence in his own ability.

At least as important as the nature of social interaction is the emphasis on criteria of achievement. Success on the job may depend in part on personal relationships, but it depends more on objective standards of skill and productivity. The strategy of men like Velasco is to meet those standards. If they do, the rules of the union and the profitability of the firm guarantee them a secure and financially rewarding future.

Upward mobility in the industrial context is a viable strategy for those with the skills, the ambition, and especially the advantage of having a job in the first place. Now that the factories are no longer expanding, the chance to move ahead in industry is available only to a very few of the increasing numbers of young people entering the labor force.

A Mixed Strategy. An extended family may draw on various occupational possibilities to form a mixed strategy. The Velascos offer one of the best examples of this kind of approach. The father is a charter member of the *ejido* where he lives and where he still holds rights in land; but he works as a maintenance man in the railroad car factory. One of the sons is a white-collar employee and the other, mentioned above, is a welder's apprentice. A son-in-law who lives in the family compound runs the farming operations, which include planting corn and barley and feeding some cattle and a flock of chickens.

Migration. Before the coming of the new town, the only way for many people of Los Llanos to adapt was to move out rather than to try to survive there at all. The entire state of Hidalgo was noted for its high rate of emigration to more industrialized areas of the country. In the Valley of Los Llanos, Ciudad Industrial reversed the procees for a time. People who could not find opportunities locally still moved out, but there were fewer in that category; and more moved in to take up jobs in the factories. Within the past few years two processes unfortunately have coincided: the expansion of industry has stopped, and the rate of population growth has increased. The rate of growth has increased because the birth rate has remained high, and the death rate has decreased. The rate of infant mortality in particular has decreased because of the diffusion of modern medicine and the use of new drugs that combat pneumonia and other diseases that often have been fatal to children. The influx of young families into the region and decreasing infant mortality have produced a bumper crop of teenagers, with even more to come.

Economic development in the Valley of Los Llanos has come full circle. Population growth has cancelled out the gains from industrialization, and unemployment is as serious a problem as it was before the new town was built. For many of the young people entering the labor market, the only alternative will be migration to metropolitan areas with higher rates of economic growth. The closest area is Mexico City. So again it is the growth of population that has undermined one of the goals of Ciudad Industrial: alleviation of the heavy concentration of industry, people, and pollution in the Federal District.

Some Questions of Policy

This book has been concerned with the efforts of people to adapt to circumstances largely beyond their control. On one hand are the constraints imposed by the environment: the vicissitudes of the weather and the poverty of natural resources. On the other hand are the important changes effected by the operation of Mexican society: the decline in the market for *pulque* resulting from changes in public tastes, and the building of the new town as a result of decisions made in national centers of power. Students of anthropology are likely to have some familiarity with environmental constraints, since the effects of the environment on the evolution of culture has been a traditional concern of the discipline. They are also likely to understand the importance of market forces, not so much from their study of anthropology, but from their culturally-derived awareness of economic factors. They are less likely to appreciate the role of public policy in effecting basic social change, so I want to place particular emphasis on this. I have not attempted to analyze the making of policy: that is the domain of political science. But I have tried to show some of the social effects of policy decisions

The Consequences of Planning. The annals of anthropology contain many examples of the unintended and unexpected consequences of small-scale technological changes; but few of these examples show the reverberating effects of large-scale development projects. Both the design of Ciudad Industrial and the policies governing its operation have contributed to the unplanned consequences. A direct effect has been the atmosphere of coldness and artificiality about which some of the residents complain. The monotony of the houses, the location of the main plaza, the strict controls over commerce, and the prohibition of saloons all affect the tone of social life and encourage the inhabitants to maintain identification with their home towns.

These same policies have had a major indirect effect: men from the villages who found jobs in the factories decided in overwhelming numbers to continue living in the villages, and growing numbers of outsiders have also settled there. Both groups have been a potent force for change, and their communities have found the prosperity denied Ciudad Industrial. In the summer of 1969, there were fifty-five new houses under construction in Benito Juárez, most of which belonged to employees of the factories. This figure represents about ten percent of the dwelling units in the community. By way of contrast, no new houses have been built in the new town for more than a decade.

The rate of population growth is perhaps the simplest indicator of the development of communities. The census figures in Table 10-1 show the impact of Ciudad Industrial on the surrounding region. The head towns of all the adjoining *municipios* appear in the table. The growth should be compared to that of the new town, which increased rapidly until the mid-1960's and which leveled off just as rapidly after that. Cerro Grande, the head town of the *municipio* in which Ciudad Industrial is located, has grown the most. Serena, in the next valley to the north, beyond the immediate sphere of the new town's influence, has grown the least.

Table 10.1. Population Growth in Head Towns
Around Ciudad Industrial

	1960	1970	Percentage of Growth During Decade
Cerro Grande	3,076	7,027	128%
Malapan	2,041	3,127	53%
Benito Juárez	2,059	3,874	88%
Los Llanos	8,640	13,705	59%
San Alvaro	913	1,218	33%

A Regional Perspective. All of the evidence points to the necessity for considering the entire region as the relevant social unit when evaluating a project such as Ciudad Industrial. The economists and planners of the *Banco de México* and *Nacional Financiera* were not involved simply with locating new factories in accord with national economic goals. They were also sensitive to political considerations about the regional distribution of the investment of federal funds, and concerned with social goals of reducing unemployment and promoting the welfare of the population. Accordingly, the new town was launched with a degree of fanfare appropriate to the great expectations held for it, but government agencies have been disappointed about its problems and its retarded development.

The question now arises: what light does the research reported in this book shed on the question of the success or failure of Ciudad Industrial? In order to comment on this question, I must first state my views about the relationship between research and evaluation and about the proper role of foreign social scientists.

Our research in the Valley of Los Llanos has been concerned with basic processes of social change stimulated in large part by the development of the new town and its factories. We have attempted to discover, and to document with both quantitative and qualitative data, the effects on the surrounding villages. The evaluation of Ciudad Industrial would be a much more complex procedure. It could draw on the results of anthropological research, but it also would require other kinds of data: for example, full knowledge of the original goals and investments, and detailed analysis of the economic status of the factories.

The evaluation of development projects in Mexico is the responsibility of the agencies that plan and conduct them and of the elected representatives of the Mexican people. It would not be appropriate for foreign anthropologists to make judgments about the success or failure of such projects. But they can contribute relevant data as part of the basis for making judgments. The results of our research in the Valley of Los Llanos demonstrate that Ciudad Industrial is having a reverberating impact on the region. For questions of policy, the most important conclusion of our research is the need to consider the region as the unit of analysis.

The Unfinished Revolution

One of the themes of this book has been the need to see the single community, that small-scale unit to which anthropologists have been devoted, in the context of the region; and the need to see the region in the context of the nation. So perhaps it is appropriate to close with some comments about Mexico in 1972.

The dominant political party in Mexico is the *Partido Revolucionario Institucional* (PRI), the "Institutional Revolutionary Party." This name reflects one of the main features of the party's ideology: the commitment to a revolution seen not as a single historical event, but rather as an institutionalized process that responds to the changing needs of society. One of the principal persisting problems of Mexico is the unequal distribution of the fruits of the Revolution. The gap between rich and poor is no wider there than in the United States; but the Mexican poor are much poorer and much more conspicuous, and the "rich" would not be considered rich by United States standards.

The current president, Luis Echeverría Alvarez, elected for the 1970-76 term, has expressed a renewed concern about persisting inequalities. The *Mexican Newsletter*, published in English by his office, stated the problem in this way on March 31, 1972:

Old inequalities have not yet been overcome. The country's Indian population lives in a consumptive economy. Neither ignorance nor hunger have been eradicated. The communications network is inadequate. Advanced agriculture coexists with rudimentary systems. The benefits of industrialization have favored only a few and the need for resources is answered with wastefulness. It is imperative that the wealth created be distributed so that it generates new wealth. Unemployment exists not as a result of the Government's social and economic policies, but in spite of them.

It is necessary to banish threats and fears derived from growing inequality. The poor must not be exposed to hunger nor the rich to a loss of their properties. The State has a vital role to play in this objective. To this end it must seek support in domestic resources rather than foreign borrowings. One of its most urgent tasks is to reduce unemployment and create new jobs.

One of the inequalities mentioned here is the growing discrepancy in employment opportunities, productivity, and standard of living between the more developed and less developed regions of the country (Hansen 1971:82-95). The great momentum of Mexico's economic growth, proudly called "the Mexican miracle," has produced a continual widening of those discrepancies. So far, the government agencies devoted to promoting industrialization have not been much concerned about questions of regional balance (Barkin and King 1970:116). *Nacional Financiera,* the largest development bank, and other agencies have concentrated on import-substitution; that is, promoting and financing the production of goods that previously had to be imported. They have used public investment in new industries as a tool of economic policy much more than of social policy. The welfare of a region or of a segment of the population has been a secondary consideration in decisions about industrial location. This is not to say that the government has neglected social concerns; on the contrary, they have been important considerations in development schemes for river basins and other projects. But Ciudad Industrial has been one of the rare efforts to use industrialization to promote the social welfare of a region.

Ciudad Industrial may turn out to be the forerunner of other efforts. The new president, Luis Echeverría Alvarez, has adopted economic decentralization and regional development as fundamental policies of his administration. The problems that the Valley of Los Llanos faced twenty years ago are being felt increasingly in villages throughout Mexico: population is rapidly outstripping resources; given present technology, agriculture has reached the limit of its potential; and the only alternative to massive migration is the development of new sources of employment in the countryside. The survival of many Mexican villages will depend on the adaptive strategies of the people within the context of policies set by the nation.

CHAPTER ELEVEN

Epilogue

Toward the end of the summer of 1972, a few days after I finished the manuscript for this book, Charles Mundale returned from a trip to Mexico. He had visited Ciudad Industrial in order to keep in touch with developments since his initial research on political organization three years before. His visit was well timed: President Echeverría was on hand to announce an important change in policy for the town and some significant developments for the factories.

The change in policy is a program of selective conversion to privately-owned housing. Both white-collar and blue-collar employees will soon have the opportunity to buy, at reasonable prices, the houses that they occupy. Those who take advantage of the opportunity will have greater latitude in creating and modifying the conditions of their domestic environment.

The developments in the factories are the most ambitious plans for expansion since they were constructed. The railroad car factory will begin immediately to assemble, for the first time, diesel locomotives to be furnished to the national railways and to be sold in Latin America and elsewhere in the world. It will also build cars for the Metro, the elegant new subway in Mexico City. In addition, construction will begin on a new factory to manufacture heavy drilling equipment for large water wells, oil wells, and such purposes; and there are longer range plans for two more industries, details of which have not been announced.

Perhaps the development that will have the most significance in the long run is the interest of the factories' new director-general in promoting a kind of cottage industry in which workers and their families would group together and subcontract with the factories for the manufacture of small parts. The goals would be to open up new opportunities for small-scale entrepreneurship and to spread more widely the economic impact of industry.

The new activities in Ciudad Industrial are only one example of the Mexican government's efforts to attack the problem of inequalities among the various regions of the country and the various segments of its population. They promise to create another round of opportunities for the people of Los Llanos, who are engaged in the continuing human struggle to survive in the face of scarce resources and to adapt to changes beyond their control.

Bibliography

Artes de México
1964 *[Ciudad Industrial] y sus Alrededores.* No. 56–57.

Aubey, Robert T.
1966 *Nacional Financiera and Mexican Industry.* Los Angeles: University of California, Latin American Center.

Barkin, David, and Timothy King
1970 *Regional Economic Development: The River Basin Approach in Mexico.* Cambridge: Cambridge University Press.

Beals, Ralph L.
1969 *Politics of Social Research.* Chicago: Aldine Publishing Co.

Benitez Zenteno, Raúl, and Gustavo Cabrera Acevedo
1966 *Proyecciones de la Población de México 1960–1980.* Mexico, D.F.: Banco de México.

Blair, Calvin P.
1964 "Nacional Financiera: Entrepreneurship in a Mixed Economy," in *Public Policy and Private Enterprise in Mexico*, Raymond Vernon (ed.). Cambridge: Harvard University Press.

Chevalier, Francois
1963 *Land and Society in Colonial Mexico: The Great Hacienda.* Berkeley: University of California Press (originally published in Paris 1952).

Cone, Cynthia A.
  1970 "Occupational Choice in an Industrializing Region." Paper presented at the Annual Meeting of the American Anthropological Association, San Diego.

Cumberland, Charles C.
  1968 *Mexico: The Struggle for Modernity*. London: Oxford University Press.

Fallers, Lloyd A.
  1964 "Equality and Inequality in Human Societies," in *Horizons of Anthropology*, Sol Tax (ed.). Chicago: Aldine Publishing Co.

Foster, George M.
  1967 *Tzintzuntzan: Mexican Peasants in a Changing World*, Boston: Little, Brown and Co.

Gold, Gerald L.
  1968 *The Commercial Complexity and Development of a Mexican Region*. Minneapolis: unpublished M.A. thesis, University of Minnesota.

González Cosío, Arturo
  1961 *"Clases y estratos sociales,"* in *México: Cincuenta Años de Revolución*, Vol. II. México, D.F.: Fondo de Cultura Económica.

Guttman, Louis
  1944 "A Basis for Scaling Qualitative Data," *American Sociological Review* 9:139–150.

Hansen, Roger D.
  1971 *The Politics of Mexican Development*. Baltimore: The Johns Hopkins Press.

Lewis, Oscar
  1951 *Life in a Mexican Village: Tepoztlán Restudied*. Urbana: University of Illinois Press.
  1961 *The Children of Sánchez*. New York: Random House.

Loyola Montemayor, Elias
  1956 *La Industria del Pulque*. México, D.F.: Banco de México.

Menzel, Herbert
1953 "A New Coefficient for Scalogram Analysis," *Public Opinion Quarterly* 17:268–280.

Miller, Frank C., and Pertti J. Pelto
n.d. *The Regional Impact of a New Industrial Town in Mexico.* In preparation.

Mintz, Sidney W., and Eric R. Wolf
1950 "An Analysis of Ritual Co-Parenthood (*Compadrazgo*)." *Southwestern Journal of Anthropology,* 6:341–368.

Mundale, Charles I.
1971 *Local Politics, Integration, and National Stability in Mexico.* Minneapolis: Unpublished Ph.D. Dissertation, University of Minnesota.

Pelto, Pertti J.
1970 *Anthropological Research: The Structure of Inquiry.* New York: Harper and Row.

Poggie, John J., Jr.
1968 *The Impact of Industrialization on a Mexican Intervillage Network.* Minneapolis: Unpublished Ph.D. dissertation, University of Minnesota.
1972 "Ciudad Industrial: A New City in Rural Mexico," in *Technology and Social Change,* H. Russell Bernard and Pertti J. Pelto (eds.). New York: Macmillan.

Poggie, John J., Jr., and Frank C. Miller
1969 "Contact, Change and Industrialization in a Network of Mexican Villages," *Human Organization* 28:190–198.

Redfield, Robert
1930 *Tepoztlán: A Mexican Village.* Chicago: University of Chicago Press.
1941 *The Folk Culture of Yucatan.* Chicago: University of Chicago Press.

Roufs, Timothy G.
1971 *Education and Occupational Aspirations in a Changing Society.* Minneapolis: Unpublished Ph.D. dissertation, University of Minnesota.

Saturday Review
    1971   "New Communities: Business on the Urban Frontier." May 15,
            Special issue.

Schensul, Jean J.
    1972   "Education in Benito Juárez: Investment for the Future."
            Unpublished manuscript.

Simon, Barbara D.
    1968   "Social Stratification in a Modern Mexican Community." Paper
            presented at the Annual Meeting of the Central States Anthro-
            pological Society, Detroit.
    1972   *Power, Privilege, and Prestige in a Mexican Town: The Impact*
            of Industry on Social Stratification. Minneapolis: Unpublished
            Ph.D. dissertation, University of Minnesota.

Stavenhagen, Rodolfo
    1970   "Social Aspects of Agrarian Structure in Mexico," in *Agrarian*
            Problems and Peasant Movements in Latin America, Rodolfo
            Stavenhagen (ed.). New York: Doubleday Anchor Books.

Tannenbaum, Frank
    1950   *Mexico: The Struggle for Peace and Bread.* New York: Alfred
            A. Knopf.

Wolf, Eric
    1955   "Types of Latin American Peasantry: A Preliminary Discus-
            sion." *American Anthropologist* 57:452–72.
    1957   "Closed Corporate Peasant Communities in Mesoamerica and
            Central Java." *Southwestern Journal of Anthropology* 13:1–18.
    1958   "The Virgin of Guadalupe: A Mexican National Symbol."
            Journal of American Folklore 71:34–38.
    1959   *Sons of the Shaking Earth.* Chicago: University of Chicago
            Press.

Yates, Paul Lamartine
    1961   *El Desarrollo Regional de México.* México, D.F.: Banco de
            México.

Young, Frank W.
    1964   "Location and Reputation in a Mexican Intervillage Network,"
            Human Organization 23:36–41.

Young, Frank W., and Ruth C.
    1960 "Social Integration and Change in Twenty-Four Mexican Villages." *Economic Development and Culture Change* 8:366–377.
    1962 "Occupational Role Perceptions in Rural Mexico." *Rural Sociology* 27:42–52.
    1966 "Individual Commitment to Industrialization in Rural Mexico." *American Journal of Sociology* 31:373–383.

Index